GREAT GHOSTS OF THE WEST

RICHARD WEBB

NASH PUBLISHING
Los Angeles

LIBRARY OF CONGRESS CATALOG CARD NUMBER: 71-124413

STANDARD BOOK NUMBER: 8402-1142-2

PUBLISHED SIMULTANEOUSLY IN THE UNITED STATES AND
CANADA BY NASH PUBLISHING, 9255 SUNSET BOULEVARD,
LOS ANGELES, CALIFORNIA 90069.

PRINTED IN THE UNITED STATES OF AMERICA

FIRST PRINTING

*To my wife, Florence, who also
believes, and who has always
helped me so much, gracias.*

Contents

Introduction

My interest in the so-called occult—the supernatural, the supernormal—goes back to the time when a boyfriend and I, both thirteen, spent a night in an old abandoned house, in a small town in Illinois. During the night something awakened us, and after we watched a garden rake walk across the room with no visible means of mobility, we took off! From that time forward my appetite was whetted to find out who, what, when, and where.

As an actor, I have traveled around the country a good deal, and I've talked with people from every walk of life, and gotten stories and anecdotes from many of them about every conceivable ghostly and occult subject. It is interesting to note that in the past few years scientific and public topics have swung more and more to the occult, continuing life, ESP. In the light of what man sees when he looks at his material progress, he understandably feels a lack, feels there must be something more. We seem to have developed a tremendous material knowledge but very little understanding of the "invisibles" which are so abundant.

When the idea of doing a book first occurred to me, I knew it would have to be written in such a manner as to attract all age groups, span generation gaps. Therefore, to span the gap with my young readers, I shall toss in some dialogue to indicate I'm not all square. don't take the oblique look at phenomena. I've scanned the scene for many years and have tried to pick up on the ghostly arrangement, blow the right sounds. Having dug my dharma, I'm now turning the whole cool gig over to the public cat!

I had to make a decision. Would I write about ghosts and occult phenomena nationally, or confine myself to a specific area? Being a resident of California, where written material about such matters is relatively sparse, I settled on my own state. By and large the stories are statewide, but being a buff of the Mojave Desert and an amateur prospector of the Sierra Nevadas, many of them are drawn from those areas.

The response I've received from groups and individuals around the country when I've brought up the subject of ghosts and the occult, ranges from the sublime to the ridiculous. A few times I've been told to leave; once I was threatened with the police; a woman called her priest to have me exorcised as I was possessed for believing such, to her, anti-Christ horrors! Along with the sublime and the ridiculous, it has been a most revealing and rewarding quest. I want to thank the many who, even though they professed unbelief, cooperated with me, told me of their experiences, and have even put me in touch with others who might have a story to add to what I'm doing now, writing about it.

Some years ago ghost stories were merely an unknown something you read about or talked about around a campfire or before the fireplace to raise chills, so that when you went to bed you would have delicious nightmares of diaphanous, sheeted figures floating through your dreams, of perfidious, loathsome old crones concocting an infernal brew, pursuing little boys and girls through dark and noisome forests and stygian caves. Mostly, those myths have given way to the maturing scientific knowledge that there is something more concerning continuing life: spirits of the departed are still around; there is no time in eternity as we know it; areas do contain memory of what happened there, and at times that memory is replayed, like a tape recording, when conditions are right. It is not all imagination during sleep when someone appears in a dream and talks with the sleeper; or the sleeper takes a long trip, sees strange new places, talks with people, some of whom they knew before that person "died."

If ghosts give us shivers, what kind of shivers and problems do we dense entities called mortals, physical humanity, give them?

What actually happens in a ghostly visitation is usually so commonplace the person experiencing it isn't aware of the out-of-the-ordinary manifestation until it is over. Not always, however. Sometimes the occurrence, manifestation, or visitation, is delicious, delightful, though sometimes traumatic, and the recipient is very aware he's experienced the so-called supernatural.

At the present time there has been no complete explanation of what is termed the paranormal. Parapsychology is defined as "the study that investigates the psychological aspect of such apparently supernatural phenomena as telepathy, clairvoyance, clairaudience, extrasensory perception." Large numbers of colleges now have their parapsychology departments given to study, recording, and if possible finding out what is going on, paranormally, scientifically. We all experience, from time to time, what is called *extrasensory perception*. We are also beginning to know and accept that it is something natural, not unnatural.

Any speculative comment of mine springs from my own experience. There are so many unfounded theories, so many emotional, imaginative fears. Supernatural or paranormal experiences mostly happen "out of the blue," and are usually not recognized for what they are because they occur so simply—delicately, if you will—in the normal course of events that they pass unnoticed, unrecognized.

The terms *paranormal, supernormal, supernatural,* indicate something which is above, beyond, strange. I like the term *natural.* Dr. J.B. Rhine, in his book, *The Reach of the Mind,* says, "No one knows what thought is. Nobody knows how consciousness is produced. There isn't even a theory." Doctors have operated on the human brain thousands of times, have never found a thought, never isolated what could be the "soul." A "ghost" is a manifestation of force, or energy. We don't know much about it, but like electricity, it's there.

A word about the malefic, the evil. There is no doubt that the possibility of attracting evil exists when one delves into the "unknown," pursuing ghosts, involving the occult. There is no cause to believe that if a person is evil in this physical life, the mere fact of his dying will be any indication the individual will change into some kind of angel. It is firmly held, and I believe, that we are the same personalities on the "other side" as we are here. I've stayed away from sabbats: witchly gatherings for obscene rites; from voodoo: the conjuring up of evil; and from Black Masses: that man-dreamed-up abomination which is actually practiced today and is the antithesis of goodness and morality. Those who seek evil will certainly attract it from those excarnates who are evil. The mediums with whom I have had sittings usually begin the session with a period of meditation during which they ask for guidance, for protection from evil, the seeking of contact with those who are not evil. "We attract what we seek." Take care.

The stories set down are of the type which made an indelible impression on the individual who experienced them, or have been related by another, handed down through the years.

Vengeful
or
Protective
Ghosts

The 9 Mile Ghost
Got Me

In 1968 I was physically attacked by the ghost of a man long dead! Some people tell of seeing a ghost; mine ran up and down me, chilling me tremendously. I experienced the sensation: I didn't see him. I can't blame the ghost because he was only protecting his property and I trespassed. If you have difficulty believing me, go with me while we dig into the background and the events leading up to my being run off.

About twenty years ago, a man named Harry lived near Lone Pine, California. (Since he is still alive and doing time for his crime, we will call him Harry.) Harry was a sort of prospector, house painter, handyman, jack-of-all-trades. He was also a known heavy drinker, which will usually help compound any mental or emotional aberrations one might be heir to. When he was drinking he was real mean.

One Friday afternoon in the late summer of 1948, after having imbibed his share of Old Rot with his compadres in the local gin mill, Harry decided to visit a miner, named MacSpreem, who worked his diggings in a place called 9 Mile Canyon, about forty miles from Lone Pine. (The turnoff road sign now reads Kennedy Meadows. It is on Route 395, between Mojave, California, and Lone Pine.) Fortifying himself for the trip with a jug of 86 proof Goodie Juice, Harry took off in his vintage Chevrolet.

By the time Harry reached Mac's mine, it was late afternoon. The bearded, rumpled, and dirty Mac greeted Harry jovially enough, and although Mac knew Harry to be a mean heavy drinker, he did appreciate a few snorts. It isn't exactly clear from the records just what the two talked about as they snapped at the jug, or what started the altercation, but a fight did ensue. Harry pulled a gun and shot MacSpreem in the head, like dead. After murdering MacSpreem, Harry—to finish his part in the proceedings—took off down 9 Mile Canyon and drove to Keeler, California, about twenty-five miles away, on the edge of Owens Dry Lake, between Lone Pine and Death Valley. There he did some more drinking with a man named Scrap Iron. They got into a fracas, Harry pulled his every-ready gun, and shot and killed Scrap Iron. Harry was subsequently caught, tried, convicted, and put in the penitentiary.

From all accounts this writer has been able to run down, Mac's claim doesn't seem to have been good enough for him to have been murdered for it. There was a little gold and silver, but there's a little gold and silver in a lot of places. The diggings have lain fallow, unworked since Mac was murdered.

In the fall of 1968, in company with my dog and driving a four-wheel drive station wagon, I headed for Lone Pine to visit my friend, Constable Jesse Covington, then to go on to Panamint Valley, east of Lone Pine, to check on a mineral location I'd been prospecting.

Having noted the Kennedy Meadows sign many times, and my curiosity getting the better of me this trip, I turned west off Highway 395 and wound my way up the nine-mile grade to the top, where once there lived about three hundred people, mostly engaged in mining. Mac's prospect is about twelve miles off the main highway, up the canyon, near a mountain called Chimney Peak, at an elevation of 6000 feet. (If you should take the trip up there, use low gear coming out; don't ride the brakes anymore than absolutely necessary because they will heat up and you'll wind up as I did—slamming the nose of the car into a hill to stop! My time hadn't come.)

It was dark when I reached the top of the grade, but I had good lights, plenty of gas, oil, and supplies. Anyhow, I wanted to try out a new fluorescent light to see if I could black lamp some minerals that can only be found in this particular manner.

I followed a dirt road about two miles, and, noting a dirt side road intersecting, turned off and drove another half mile. As the road took a slight curve, my headlights picked up what appeared to be a depression off to one side. I'd not previously checked any maps, had no knowledge of any mines in the area, nor did I see any evidence of digging.

There was no other conscious reason why I decided to stop and take a look. It was about 11 P.M. I opened the wagon door and my dog jumped out, followed by me, armed with a rock hammer, the black lamp, and a .38 Smith & Wesson revolver I sometimes carry when I'm out in the remote desert areas. I snapped the black lamp on and began walking slowly toward the rock-strewn depression, the lamp casting its ultraviolet rays about three feet ahead of me.

Not until I approached to within some ten feet of the depression did I become aware of anything unusual, and that came with a rush. Suddenly, I was seized with the biggest chill I ever remember experiencing. It started on the back of my neck and zipped down over my lower body—jerked me upright. At once the boyhood memories of cemeteries, moonless nights in the woods, ghosts, all came flooding back. My first and natural inclination was to run! Quickly, I turned on the flashlight portion of the black lamp and swept it about. My dog, prowling about doing his own prospecting, didn't seem bothered or aware of anything out of the ordinary. I forced myself to stop being afraid, and I turned on the black lamp and began searching once more. Within another twenty seconds that tremendous chill seized me again. This one seemed to rush at me from behind, engulfing my whole back, shoulders and neck. Let's say it stopped me cold! I snapped on the flashlight again. Nothing was moving, present or evident, except my dog. Once again I fought down that wild desire to run. Again I turned on the black lamp, forcing myself to continue. Again, that chill blast hit me.

This time there was no doubt in my mind. Something physical was there.

Quickly I snapped on the flashlight, pulled my .38, holding it ready, began backing up—hurriedly I might add—calling my dog to get into the station wagon. It wasn't until I'd driven three or four miles from that spot that I calmed down enough to pull over, lock all the doors, stretch out on the mattress in the back section, and try to get some sleep, using the gun as a pillow.

The following morning as I drove back out, I passed the benighted depression, and it seemed peaceful enough—not a soul around, the ground not disturbed, nothing. Secretly I felt I'd given way to imagination, but the literal terror of the unnamed, the unknown, those chills, the feeling that something or someone had been present remained startlingly clear. I shuddered in the most approved manner as I passed the spot.

After driving to Lone Pine, I went directly to my lawman friend's house. It sits unobtrusively next door to the Lone Pine high school. Jesse was home, and after his wife had fixed us each a cup of java, we sat down at the kitchen table to chin a bit. It didn't take me long to get around to my experience of the previous night. I'd known Jesse for some years, but it was still a bit shamefacedly that I recited my ghostly visitation, admitted it had scared me stiff. After I'd finished, he smiled.

"That's old Mac!"

"What do you mean 'old Mac'?"

He then told me how Mac had met his end, and added that I was probably the fifteenth or twentieth person who'd come in and reported the exact same incident from the same location!

In the intervening time, I've read dozens of books on ghosts, hauntings, witchings, materializations, physical manifestations—you name it—in an attempt to acquaint myself with the kinds of phenomena that are so widely reported from around our planet. I've talked with those to whom "things" have happened; with priests who've exorcised houses, and with people who were "haunted" or possessed. Everyone knowledgeable on the subject admits, agrees, and attests to the fact that we are not alone here on earth, but probably interpenetrated by the invisible spirits of those who've passed on, died. The spirits can see us, some dimly, some clearly. From the information gathered from psychics and mediums, we are more dense and can't see spirits unless they materialize, but we can and do *feel* their presence.

There is a mountain of evidence on the existence of discarnate or excarnate entities, and that evidence is mounting daily. Discarnate spirits are those who have never been born into earthly life, so "they" tell us. Excarnate spirits are those who have lived on this earth and who, having died, are still earthbound, here among us, so they tell us—and show us!

When the world-reknowned trance-medium, Reverend Arthur Ford, was in California recently on a lecture tour, I invited him to my house for dinner. In our discussions I brought up the incident of old Mac. Mr. Ford told me the phenomenon is not unusual—that is, until it happens to an individual unaccustomed to it, with which I heartily agreed! The reverend added that should I, or anyone else, be interested enough to go back, contact old Mac, or wait for Mac to contact us, we should sit down, without fear (?), and try to convince Mac he is no longer in the physical life. Mac must now progress himself, shake off the mundane earthly things, and gain knowledge of where he is and how he can learn the new lessons in spirit life, those things which await us earthlings when we shuffle off this mortal coil.

No, I've not gone back as yet, although I have a number of friends who want to go with me to see if we can convince Mac to leave. Right now he's undoubtedly busy chilling people off his mining claim in the only manner he knows.

If you don't take my word for it and if you ever go to Lone Pine, California, stop in and talk with Jesse Covington. You might even want to go up to Kennedy Meadows and try it for yourself. Should you go up and see some guy sitting out in the open, in a little depression, shaking, seemingly talking to himself, it'll probably be me, trying to talk old Mac into leaving!

Now that we are getting into the ghostly vignettes, it will be good for our purpose to have an understanding of the semantics — just what we mean when we use certain words or phrases. I draw upon scientific expertise and research evidence for the following:

Clairvoyance: A power of discerning objects or happenings

which are not evident to the normal senses. Keen perception; great insight.

Clairaudience: The audible hearing of an inner voice or other sounds, without the use of the physical ears.

Telepathy: Supposed communication between minds by some means other than the normal sensory channels; transference of thought.

Precognition: Previous knowledge of future events.

Psychokinesis (Telekinesis): The movement of an object not in contact with the body generating the force; supposedly caused by spiritualistic or spiritistic methods.

Retrocognition: Knowledge of past events; past lives.

Trance: A state during which the conscious mind rests, while the psychic mind is given free rein.

Apports: Movement of objects by so-called supernormal means; at times from great distances and through locked doors, stone walls, etc.

Automatic Writing: Writing purported to be coming from the deep subconscious, or from someone on the other side.

Psychometry: Mysterious subjective knowledge drawn from contact with objects belonging to or used by some other person.

Levitation: The rising of the body or objects by no visible means of support.

Spirit Control (Guide): An excarnate, or discarnate (former mortal) who serves as a kind of go-between for the trance medium, or conscious medium, and living entities, who allegedly relay messages from those on the other side.

Ghosts (Poltergeist): Disembodied souls; the soul or spirit of a deceased person conceived either as a denizen of the world or as appearing to the living in bodily likeness; specter, spook.

Aura: Radiation said to surround every object, particularly from human bodies, and capable of being seen by many 'sensitives' (psychics or mediums).

Ectoplasm: In spiritualism, the emanation from a medium which apparently produces motion in distant objects without the use of physical contact.

Astral Projection: The projection of the ethereal body (soul, spirit) during either waking or sleeping, during which the astral body is separate from the physical body. Also *Teleportation* or *Bilocation:* To be transported to a distant place by spirit. The physical body is not transported; it is the astral body.

Deja Vu: The feeling that you have been somewhere, or done something before. A "familiar" feeling.

Possession: Fact or fiction state of being dominated by an extraneous personality, a demon, passion, idea, or the like.

Clairsentience: A "hunch," that peculiar feeling that something is going to happen.

Exorcism: Expulsion of malevolent spirits from possessed persons or places.

Glossolaly (Xenoglossis): The talk of an entranced medium in languages with which they are not familiar in their conscious state.

Reincarnation: The belief that the spirit of a deceased person will incarnate again in another physical body. this is not the same as *Metempsychosis,* the doctrine that the psyche (astral body) of a deceased person will attach itself to the spirit of a living person; nor is it the same as *Transmigration,* which teaches that the spirit of a deceased person will transmigrate into the body of an animal.

Medium: A person who acts as intermediary for communication between the material world and the spirit world.

Table turning, Spirit Rapping: Tilts, knocks, raps, usually in reply to questions asked by a living person, and answered in this manner by those on the other side.

In the 1860's, psychic phenomena became a scientific study, due largely to the efforts of that savant, F.W.H. Myers, who spent thirty years in research and then another ten years writing his book *Human Personality and Its Survival of Bodily Death.* Myers is looked upon as the father of modern psychic research. Since his death in 1901, the wealth of psychic material recorded, tested, and authenticated by some of the best scientific research minds of this planet is more than abundant and is mounting daily.

The incarnate (living) human being, in its dense physical body, is said to be composed of three levels of consciousness: (1) *The superconscious mind* is like our guardian, in the sense that when the conscious and the subconscious minds, in let us say, an extremity, need assistance, then the superconscious can be called upon for help in both direction and memory; otherwise the superconscious knows all about us, allows us to work out our own problems. It is sometimes referred to as the *high self.* (2) *The conscious mind* is our directive level, which guides us to do, to think, to choose. It has no memory. (3) *The subconscious mind,* having been given direction by the conscious mind, calls upon memory and supplies answers to questions, or directions fed it by the conscious mind. The subconscious mind has no direction, but does contain all race and life memory. It is sometimes referred to as the *low self.*

From all the evidence, it seems the discarnate or excarnate spirits manifest or work through the subconscious mind, and when felt or seen, do so by way of the conscious mind. Now, what if the conscious mind is removed from the subconscious mind, cut off, separated in some manner, as is the case with old MacSpreem? The conscious mind was shot away. His sub-conscious mind doesn't know he can leave, has no direction, just memory. That is why it is believed, and proven, that a living physical being, having a conscious directive mind, could possibly "direct" Mac to leave.

The Dead Finger
Points

Mt. Breckenridge, California, in the High Sierras, elevation 7,544 feet, had been a logging camp for many years, and still is. It is reached from Bakersfield, California, by taking Walker Pass into the town of Kernville, and from there on, the logger's road into the high reaches of Breckenridge. Its lumber camp has been supplying timber for the mills as far away as Los Angeles, some one hundred and fifty miles, for many years. Daily, the huge trucks rumble out loaded with the stately pine. In 1960, when I was starring in the TV series, "U.S. Border Patrol," for CBS-TV, we made four of the shows up there, in Kernville, and at the Mt. Breckenridge camp. The story was told me at that time, and I wrote it up and placed it in my files. The old Kernville area is now under water due to the creation of the popular summer resort known as Lake Isabella. Kernville, as the old-timers would remember it, was originally called Whiskey Flat, a rough, tough, mining, logging, and cattle town much given to violence, revelry, and ribaldry.

Shortly after the turn of the century, the loggers at Mt. Breckenridge had employed a Chinese cook called Wong. He hailed from San Francisco, by way of Hong Kong.

Wong was a handsome man, well-spoken, and a darned good cook. One day, one of the married women, fairly well in her cups, entered the camp kitchen where Wong was finishing preparations for lunch. The tables were all set; it was right at noon. The lady must have felt sexily playful that day because she made a nuisance of herself by making advances to Wong, who would have nothing to do with her. Enraged at being thusly rejected by, to her, such an inferior individual, the spruned female rent her clothing, ran outside, and set up a hue and cry about Wong, attempting to rape her.

The loggers, already on their way to the mess hall, swarmed in and grabbed the unfortunate Wong, and without as much as a by-your-leave, dragged him outside and strung him to a convenient tree. While he was still kicking out the last of his earthly life, the five participants trooped back into the mess hall, sat down, and ate the meal he'd prepared.

Ultimately, word of the hanging filtered out to San Francisco, to the Chinese Embassy, and the Chinese government made inquiries of the American government in Washington. A half-hearted investigation was conducted, but the Breckenridgites clamped a tight lid of silence on the whole affair, didn't know anything about it. After all, in those days, what was the life of mere Chinese cook worth? It was finally agreed between the two governments that it had been an unfortunate incident, and the case was closed. Attempted rape is a charge easy to make, hard to prove, and harder to defend, and the woman remained adamant in her assertions about Wong. Chinese were expendable.

Particularly in those days, the Chinese tongs in San Francisco were pretty powerful organizations, at least among the Chinese. They were on the order of unions of today. They kept track of their countrymen the best they could, being the clearinghouse for their entry into the United States, helping them find jobs, for a price, and seeing that their bodies were returned to China for burial, whenever possible, again, for a price.

Some months after the incident, five Chinese showed up in Mt. Breckenridge. They didn't seem to be looking for jobs, had enough money to support themselves, and stayed away from the whites. They were members of the tong their deceased countryman had belonged to; and they were out for retribution. The whites began asking questions of them but could get no satisfactory answers, just polite evasion, as befitted the inscrutable Oriental.

The tong members had no way of actually knowing who had been in on the hanging, and when their presence as tongs became known to the loggers, the wall of silence from the whites went up even higher and thicker. Of the fifty loggers and their families, five men had been a party to the murder of Wong, that is all the tongs found out in their investigation.

The story of how the tong members identified and disposed of the five hangmen wasn't known, but disappear they did, one at a time, no muss, no fuss, nothing, gone. There were never any mistakes. The camp was in a turmoil, as can be imagined. The U.S. Marshal was sent for, charges were hurled at the tongs, but no evidence was ever found to connect the tongs with the disappearances.

The tongs were watched carefully, and fearfully. They didn't overtly do anything to arouse the inhabitants, and you can't stop people from walking around, keeping mostly to themselves, staying in their place as the saying goes.

Some of the loggers and their families moved clear out of Camp Breckenridge, although they'd had nothing to do with the hanging. I guess their consciences bothered them because they knew who had done the deed; and anyway, some of the loggers were accusing each other of ratting to the tongs, and bloodshed had become frequent. The camp truly became a place a man wouldn't want his kids in, or himself for that matter, guilty or innocent.

Over a period of six months, all five of the men involved disappeared. They'd not moved, just were gone, while their families remained. No trace of bodies or graves was ever found, and to this day, no sign of their remains has been turned up.

When the last of the five had been accounted for, the general manager of the logging operation encountered one of the Chinese tong members and made the remark, "Those were the five who did it."

The tong replied, "Yes, I wonder what happened to them?"

Within a few days, the tongs quietly packed up and left, and life went on pretty much the way it had, and still does today on Mt. Breckenridge.

Twenty years after the Chinese had closed the incident in their own way, the method of identification of the guilty was revealed. It came through a man who'd been a logger at the time, who'd been studying to become an attorney. After the budding lawyer passed the State Bar, he practiced law in San Francisco for many years, became friendly with one of the tong members, now a man of about seventy-five, who'd been present during the Mt. Breckenridge affair. The lawyer had performed some friendly legal act for the tong, and after an oath of secrecy, the old man let him in on the secret that had been so closely guarded.

One member of the tong group was a psychic. He'd been taken along because he could "pick up" impressions of places and people. In walking about the logging camp, the ghost of the murdered Wong would appear to the psychic, point out a man who had been in on his hanging. One by one the five men disappeared. The manner in which they were disposed of was never known.

Today the unsuspecting public romps, hunts, and fishes all over the area, little aware that they may be skipping over the graves of men who were pointed out to a clairvoyant by the dead finger of Wong, who'd hung around long enough to see his murderers disposed of.

Nothing is known of the woman who caused the violence in the first place, except that she was one of the first to pull out of camp when the tongs showed up. If the ghost of the vilified Wong was this much in evidence, he probably had his own method of harrassing her, and who knows how she got it in the end?

This Place Is
Mine

On November 6, 1969, a motion picture company happened to be making a movie at the poor farm, alongside Highway 395. As I drove out of Bridgeport, California, heading south for Los Angeles, I noted a group of trucks and other vehicles parked about two hundred yards off the highway. Having been in the picture industry for quite a number of years, I recognized them as studio equipment and rolling stock. The studios have developed their own peculiar configurations identifying the vehicles which house the various camera and sound gear, properties, and wardrobe.

Turning off, I drove down an old, overgrown, ill-defined path, parked the car, and walked over to a group of people clustered about what once had been a barn but was now a wreck and ruin. There was the camera, the director, the actors in western garb, and the others who comprise a shooting company. Actor Jim Davis, whom I've known for many years, was starring in an opus that was recently released. We greeted each other noisily, and when I told Jim what I was doing up in that part of the country, hunting ghost stories, he immediately called a fellow over who lives up there in the back country and makes his living guiding parties into the high mountains on hunting and fishing trips. Yep, the man had a story.

Before the turn of the century, a man who everyone thought to be a remittance man (one living in a remote area or a foreign country and supported by a family, business associates, or friends who wanted him out of the way for one reason or another) lived back up near Green Lake, about fifteen miles off the highway at an elevation of 7,000 feet. He seemed well-educated, had money enough to support himself, was crippled, and walked with two canes, all bent over. In the thirty-eight years he lived there, he always lived alone, but many hunters, trappers, and cattlemen would stop by his cabin for a cup of coffee, to chin a bit, or perhaps stay the night. Though he never talked about his past life, he was always interested in what was happening, what was new.

One day in 1906, some hunters approached the cabin and called out to him. There was no answer. They looked in through a window on the side of the cabin and saw a body lying on the floor. Upon breaking in, they found it was the old gentleman. He'd been dead quite some time. They hauled him out and buried him in Bridgeport Cemetery. His personal effects included some letters addressed to him from England, Australia, and from within the United States. One of the men wrote to the people who'd signed the letters, provided there was a return address. No reply was ever received.

The cabin remained empty for many years. Later, an outfit who called themselves the Green Lake Pack Station, moved into the area about a mile from the cabin. One evening a fellow from this outfit was bringing some horses up to the station, and when he was approaching the deserted property, he was accosted by a loud voice, saying, "Whoa, whoa! Hold up there. Where are you going?" The man sat his horse, looking around, asking, "Who is it? Where are you?" The disembodied voice answered with, "You've gone far enough. What are you doing here?" He dismounted and walked all over the place trying to find out what was going on. He suspected he was being kidded by his friends from the station, just not believing what his ears had heard. Whether the horses sensed the man's fear, or heard the voice, too, isn't known, but they did a lot of shying and bucking, obviously feeling uneasy. Finally the rider remounted and rode on to the pack station to relate his experience, which added an anecdote to the mystery and to the legend.

A couple of months later, the same type thing happened to another fellow who was out hunting and was walking back up to the pack station. The voice stopped him with, "What are you doing here? What do you want?" This man, as did his friend, checked all about to find out who was doing the talking. He had no luck, either.

This phenomenon has happened four or five times in the past fifteen years, reported by reputable persons who didn't know the story about the place. Individuals going into the area of the abandoned cabin have been brought up short by the voice demanding to know who they were and what they wanted there.

It seems that, as with old MacSpreem up in Kennedy Meadows, the excarnate spirit still remains bound to his former "haunt"; but in this case he can talk. Old Mac buzzes people.

We've covered a period of about sixty-three years since the old man's death. If someone had been pulling a trick on the first man to hear the voice, whoever started it as a gag, must have handed it down from generation to generation, and it's become a running family matter!

Sometime, if you're driving through or vacationing in the Bridgeport area, ask the whereabouts of the Green Lake Pack Station, get directions to the old cabin, hang around for a while, and see if "the voice" will want to know who you are, why you are there. Drop me a line, tell me what happened.

"I'll Get You"

Most of the ghost stories I've ever heard, prior to getting into them as a fascinating study, were concerned with the scary, or horror aspect. It was quite some time and after a good deal of research before I didn't jump, pimple up, and frankly get hair-raising scared when investigating ghosts or stories about them. This next is one of those stories of the excarnate who takes furious revenge, of the retribution I'd always heard attributed to ghosts, taken upon living mortals. It is told by John Sturgeon, whose sister, Grace, relates "Bird of Ill Omen" in the second chapter.

"The Lucky Boy mine up there in Bodie shut down. There were only four or five people who stayed on after it closed. Ed and his wife, and maybe three or four more, including me. Those others were awfully heavy drinkers. Ed's wife was a Yakima Indian from Washington. She and Ed would put on some real shows sometimes when they got drunk.

"The two of them threw a real big drunk one night, and Ed shot her around five or six o'clock. He shot her in the back of the right arm, and it tore her right breast off. They had to send clear to Mina (Nevada) for a doctor, and the man who went for him only had an old horse. It took him maybe two hours to get to Hawthorne, Nevada, where they did have a telephone to call the doctor. They got hold of Doc Pash. He came over from Mina with a team and a wagon, to the Lucky Boy. They rigged up the kitchen for an operating room, and took her arm off right here [between elbow and shoulder], right there on the kitchen table.

"We got some bedsprings and a mattress and made her a bed in the back of Doc's wagon. Then we took her down the mountain, clear to Reno, to the hospital. When we got to the hospital, by golly, that woman got up out of the wagon and walked into the hospital by herself! Anyhow, the Doc came out about an hour later and told us she was dead.

"We went back up to Bodie and told them she was dead. Three of the fellows were so mad at Ed for what he had done, they took him out and strung him up to the branch of a tree over the creek up there. He kept hollerin' 'I'll get you for this.' When they swung him out over the water, he hung there for a little while, then the rope broke and he fell in the water.

"His hands were tied behind him and he was struggling around, so some of the boys went alongside him and kept pushing his head under, kicking him in the head. All that finally did him in, and he died. They hauled him out then, and buried him up on the mountain. They didn't even put a marker to show where he is."

That could have been the end of the story, and I was on tenterhooks for fear he would stop there, but thank goodness he continued!

"Well, one night, oh, a couple of months later, I guess, one of the fellows who was in on the hanging and helping Ed to die in the water, came to the bunkhouse where we were staying. He was a bit drunk, and talking a mile a minute. He said he had seen Ed on the road as he went to his cabin, and Ed made a mean face at him, shook his fist, like that, at him. The guy was sure something bad was going to happen. It did.

In a couple of days they found him lying outside his cabin, dead. It looked like he'd gotten drunk and fallen on his head on a rock. There was a big gash in his head. He was buried in the cemetery.

"Guess it was a week later when they found the second fellow sitting in a chair in his kitchen, and he was dead, too. We hooked up the wagon and took him down to Hawthorne, and a guy who had studied medicine, he said, thought because of how his face was all blown up, and his eyes, from blood, that he died from a hemorrhage in the head.

"The other guy, the third one, who helped string Ed up, and who kicked him in the head, he came running in one day and said he'd seen Ed on the road while he was riding out of town, and Ed looked at him real mean. This guy wasn't drinking, and he was crying, like a little boy. That night he disappeared. Maybe he took off after dark, but his horse was still there. We didn't ever see him again. I don't know what happened to him."

Aside from the story of the Chinese, Wong, who pointed out his killers to the tong members from San Francisco, this is the only one I've heard where a spirit entity might have had a hand in "doing in" his tormentors, or attackers. It is said that we are much the same people on the "other side" as we are while here. When we first awaken in those new surroundings, we have nothing but memory, and that memory is concerned with living in the earthly, physical body, with the things that happened prior to our physical death.

There was a man in my house recently, who came primarily to discuss a phenomenon that took place when his son and some friends used the Ouija board. Seems the young people, in a spirit of fun, challenged the board to bring through the

devil, if there was a devil! They kept their hands on the planchette, and shortly an ashtray sitting on the table they were
using shattered to bits, getting glass all over them. Following
closely upon that manifestation, they heard heavy, labored
breathing in the hall, about ten feet from them. When they
investigated they found nothing. What the man wanted to
know from me was, can this actually be true? From my own
sittings, readings, and discussions with recognized, reputable
psychics and mediums about the country, I gave him a quali-
fied yes. If Arthur Ford, the country's foremost trance
medium, in silent meditation, asks for help, for guidance, and
protection from evil before he does any trance work, that is
good enough for me. I find a parallel here with playing
around with hypnotism as a parlor game. It has been proven
beyond doubt that there is great danger in employing hypnotism unless it is done under strict conditions and pre-
ferably by a psychiatrist, psychologist, or one highly trained
to cope with any situation which might arise during the session. That situation can be one of psychotic release in the
individual.

We don't know what is buried deep in any person, and to
toy with releasing something which hypnotism might possibly do is courting disaster for the individual or those around
him. Evil entities on the other side wait their chance for such
an opportunity, and sometimes take full advantage of it. I
have a psychologist friend who absolutely refuses to use
hypnotism unless the patient is in a hospital, with attendants
nearby in case anything untoward happens which he can't
handle, like the release of multiple personality, which personalities have been known to start fighting among themselves!

"I Want You with Me"

Psychomancy: "The influence one soul is supposed to exert upon another soul," (Webster). This interesting case of the manifestation of continuing life, continuing personality, and its effect upon another is happening right now to a young lady who is the friend of a man and wife who work in the real estate office with my wife, Florence.

The young lady, Pearl, is the recipient of the phenomenon. She came into the office to visit her two friends. Although in the bloom of youth, in her early thirties, she was prematurely aging, her step was slow, her body sagging, shoulders and back bending; what should be the young, vital look in her eyes had given way to the lacklustre look of sick people twice her age. Her outward condition was so pronounced that after having been introduced to her, Florence drew the wife to one side and asked what in the world was the matter with her. The woman told her there was nothing that doctors could find physically wrong, that psychiatrists had practically given up on her and then the bomb, that it was thought she was being invaded by the excarnate spirit of her dead husband!

Immediately sensing a possible ghost story, Florence suggested they all go out for a coffee break. Working in the same office, both the man and wife had heard Florence mention I was writing a book on ghosts of California, and Florence told the wife this could be one of them, with the participants remaining anonymous. Sitting in the coffee shop, the wife led the conversation around to the subject by inquiring how Pearl felt, which gave rise to Florence explaining her interest in the ghostly aspect and asking her if she would like to talk about it. Pearl wasn't backward in discussing it. She frankly said she was sure she was being invaded by the spirit of her ex-husband. Pearl had been widowed about a year and a half ago. Her deceased husband had been the type who demanded constant attention from her. Shortly after their marriage, he began to complain of various aches and pains for which doctors could find no physical cause. Pains in the chest, pains in the head, pains in the back. Finally psychiatry was resorted to, and their report was "anxiety syndrome, with excessive dependency." That Pearl was the object of the dependency was quite obvious. During particularly the last months of his life, he demanded that Pearl be near him at all times. He would even call for her if she merely left the room to prepare food; she had to be in sight at all times.

Nothing medical or psychiatrically supportive seemed to have any effect, and the man's condition worsened week by week. He succumbed, ultimately, to a cerebral hemorrhage.

After his death, Pearl, released from the actual bondage she'd been held in, took a vacation, traveling to Oregon, New Mexico, and Northern California. About eight months later she met a man her own age and they began seeing a good deal of each other. In about three months the boyfriend popped the question, and they were married. That should be the happy ending of the story, but it was only the beginning of a downhill slide for Pearl.

Within a few months after their marriage, Pearl began to

talk in her sleep. She seemed to be holding long, and sometimes furious and tearful, conversations with someone. The new husband, deeply and rightly concerned, would awaken her and inquire what kind of nightmare she was having, and whom she was talking to in her sleep. At first she tried to pass it off as merely dreams; she begged him to be patient with her, telling him frankly that the dreams were about her former husband who appeared to her, crying pitiably, as he had done in life, calling for her, demanding she come to him. It wasn't long before Pearl began to complain of aches and pains in her back; her head would throb horribly. The same round of doctors was made by her as had been made by the ex-husband, and with the same results; nothing physical was wrong, and psychiatric sessions produced no long-term relief. The opinion of the medical men was that she suffered from psychosomatic guilt with resultant anxiety, and that there was nothing further they could do for her, except administer shock treatments. They were baffled.

Her new husband traveled a good deal for his company, and just prior to his last trip had told her they should buy a house. Perhaps that would give her an outlet, something different to do to occupy her mind. This had been one of her purposes in visiting the real estate office that day—to see her friends and get some information on houses for sale.

It would have been impossible for Florence to take enough notes to fill in the story properly, and she asked the three of them if they would like to come have dinner with us. A date was set for the following week. When Florence told me of the situation, that they were coming to talk about the phenomenon, I was pleased, but certainly disturbed! Getting involved in something like this could be dangerous, very dangerous. If that excarnate husband was truly following Pearl about, not letting her out of his sight, he quite possibly would be present when she came to the house, and there was no telling what his reaction would be to someone meddling in his personal affairs. I am not adept at tilting with spirits! We decided to go ahead with it anyway, ready to knock it off the moment he seemed to be present. I didn't want to borrow trouble—not that kind of trouble.

The three showed up on the appointed night. We had dinner and talked of various other things while, frankly, I tried to ascertain if the unwanted guest was present—the invisible sixth. There was no indication. Later, the table cleared off, we got down to the nitty-gritty. It was agreeable with Pearl that I use my tape recorder, that indispensable aid when every nuance and reference should be kept for inclusion in stories of this type.

This night, to look at her, it was hard to believe the things I'd been told about her physical condition. She was very attractive, walked straight and with vitality, her eyes bright and clear.

Here is Pearl's story as I recorded it. December 16, 1969, 9:34 P.M.

"The first time it happened, the dream, I thought it was just a dream. Gary, my husband then, appeared to me, just as he had been in life. He was calling to me, and I heard him say it, 'Pearl, you went away from me, why? I want you with me.' It woke me up. I just thought it was a holdover from before.

"Then it began to happen almost every night, even when I would take a nap in the afternoon. I would be awakened by my present husband shaking me, when it happened at night, asking me what I was talking about, who I was talking to. I told him what I could, and we both thought it was just dreams, hoped it was. Then, one night I dreamed Gary was sitting on the edge of the bed talking to me. I woke up, and Gary was sitting there! He was dressed in his street clothes, not in pajamas and robe. I saw him just as plain as I see you. It scared me so bad I screamed, I guess, because my husband woke up and wanted to know what I was yelling about? Gary disappeared. All I could do was tell what I had seen, what had happened.

"A few nights later, I had the same dream, woke up, and Gary was sitting in a chair we had right near the bed. He was crying, and saying, 'Pearl, you must come to me. I can't stand it without you, please come to me.' I shook my husband, woke him up. I told him that Gary was in the room with us, in the chair. He got up and went over toward it and Gary looked at me and said, 'Don't do that, Pearl. I love you.' Then he disappeared.

"One of the times he came to me, in the night, he said that I would have the same things happen to me that he had had, that he would get me to come to him that way. I did begin to have pains, like he did. We went to the doctors and to the psychiatrists, but they couldn't find anything wrong with me. I told them of the dreams, of Gary appearing to me, but they couldn't do anything about it. I don't know what to do. I guess they all think I'm crazy, or going crazy. Gary is there. He always did have his way, and he's having it now."

I let the machine continue to run. The room was completely quiet. The girl friend opened her mouth to speak, and I motioned her to be silent. If there was to be any manifestation of the departed Gary, I wanted to record either it or the reactions of those in the room to whatever might happen. Nothing. We sat there for about four or five minutes, silent, waiting. I turned the recorder off. If Gary hadn't manifested after what had just been told, he wasn't going to, I hoped!

Now the transition took place! I couldn't record it. Pearl began to rub her head and cry quietly. Florence got her another cup of coffee. We watched that girl revert to what they told me she was becoming, a sick old woman. Her face seemed to sag. She was moaning and rubbing her head. I turned the recorder on again just in case there was some sound or movement. Something not visible might be picked up. Pearl got up and walked toward the bathroom. She was shuffling now, as though she'd aged greatly in the past twenty minutes. There was no sound but her sobbing and shuffling. There was nothing more. Gary did not appear, nor did we hear any voice.

There you have it. Gary completely possessed Pearl during earthly life, and he is doing the same thing now as an excarnate. I have read of phenomena of this type, where there has been exorcism by a priest, and it's been sometimes successful. Hypnotism has been helpful in removing or blocking the channel from the excarnate to the incarnate; they are both possibilities. It is well and good to tell another person so afflicted they should be strong, do this, do that, and sometimes it works; but Pearl's invasion by Gary has, so far, defied analysis and supportive psychiatric help.

F.W.H. Myers, the father of modern psychical research, in his comprehensive work, *Human Personality and Its Survival of Bodily Death,* pages 26–75, deals with "Disintegrations of Personality" in just such manner as is happening to Pearl. My own possible contribution to her was to recommend she become familiar with the published works on this type phenomenon so that she could perhaps ward off Gary before he accomplished his ultimate aim of destroying her physically so she would have to join him.

Gary is miserable and unhappy where he presently is. He was miserable and unhappy here. He has, so far, been unable to learn the lesson he came into earthly life to learn, and he refuses to progress now that he is released from the physical body. How long Pearl can withstand his onslaughts is probably just a question of time, perhaps only a short time. Physically she is going downhill; it is affecting her mentally. Whether sittings with trance mediums like Arthur Ford, or clairvoyants like George Daisley, would help by having direct conversations with Gary is hard to say. Somehow Gary must be convinced that he is through with the earthly plane. His present mission should be one of help, not hindrance; he should not hold up either his or Pearl's progress by hanging around and trying to get her to join him before it is time for her to go. He is compounding the interest on the future misery he is laying up for himself.

Pearl wanted to come back again for other discussions on her problem, but I told her I just couldn't continue it; that I was not an expert, and would not, nay, could not accept the responsibility. I'd given her what knowledge and experience I had, and it would be safer and assuredly more advisable to seek a sitting with the aforementioned psychics, attempt exorcism rites by a priest, or try hypnotism under the control of psychiatric experts.

(Subsequent word from Pearl, now in England: she has contacted the Society for Psychical Research and will have meetings with them. Also, she has set up a meeting with Ena Twigg, and will let me know how things progress as she tries to convince Gary to let her alone.)

Ghostly
Warnings

"We've Come for You"

This story of departed, loving friends and relatives showing continuing love, knowledge of, and closeness to the living was related to me while I was on location with the motion picture *Out Of The Past,* starring Robert Mitchum in 1946.

To me, the lovely Sierra mountain town of Bridgeport, California, twenty-six miles down from the old ghost town of Bodie, could be my home for the rest of my earthly days. That is, summer days! At an elevation of 6,400 feet, winter temperatures can go down to fifty degrees below zero. The pass Bridgeport is situated in, is a venturi tube; the frigid air and blizzards shriek through it. The souls who live there year around are hardy, most of them third- and fourth-generation descendants of the original inhabitants. The population in the winter-locked months is about five hundred, counting dogs; the summer population, exploded by the invasion of tourists from all parts of the country approaches and many times exceeds ten thousand. Thousands more just pass through, stop for gas, or dine in the excellent restaurants. Bridgeport is the Mono county seat and the location in which this story took place.

An elderly gentleman, Walter, had lived in Bridgeport for fifty of his ninety years, and now age and a faltering heart were numbering his days. The local doctor had been able through every medical effort to keep him going but the last heart session had been extra severe and he'd been moved to the hospital, which in 1946 was in a frame building on a side street. During this last inning, the doctor said that only he and Walter were present in the little hospital room that night. The doc was sitting close to Walter's bed, doing what he could under the circumstances. Medical science can prolong life at times but when a man's time comes, he usually goes. There is a time for living, a time for dying.

All was quiet in the room; then the old man began to mutter. The doctor took his hand and bent down to hear what he was saying. Then, according to the doctor, something strange and unexplainable happened.

"Suddenly the room seemed to fill up. I felt like I was hemmed in by people, a lot of people, they crowded in. Old Walter's eyes were open, and tears were coming down his cheeks. His hand clasped mine, and his voice was low, but I distinctly heard him say, 'No, no, Robert, I don't want to go now. Not yet.' It was a pleading sob."

The doctor stroked the frail hand. "It's alright, Walter, you're not going anywhere. I'm here with you."

The old man's eyes flicked to him. "They want me to go with them. I don't want to go." Walter looked out past the doctor, and spoke to the packed silence. "No, I'll stay here with the doctor. He'll take care of me." The eyes closed, and tears trickled down the sunken cheeks.

"I just stood there, holding his hand. I've been at the bedside of a lot of patients who were dying, but this one was different. I was having chills, they ran up and down me.

Something was going on I wasn't familiar with. After about five minutes he opened his eyes again and looked out beyond me as though seeing someone. I turned my head to see if anyone had actually come in. The room was empty, but I knew we were not alone."

"Walter's voice was steadier this time. 'Alright, Edna, I'll go now, I'm ready. Yes.'

"Those were the last words he uttered in this life. the eyes closed, briefly, then opened again. The pain, the fear, had left them. He was almost smiling. Breathing became almost normal. The doctor continued to stand beside Walter, their hands clasped. Walter's eyes closed, slowly, his breathing was more and more gently shallow, just seemed to fade away, then quietly ceased.

"I was so enthralled at the phenomenon I was sure I was experiencing that I just stood there holding his limp hand. There was nothing human I could possibly do for him. It all seemed so natural and peaceful. I applied my stethoscope to his chest and could detect no breath or heart function. Then the room seemed to suddenly brighten up, get lighter, as if all the presences I'd felt were leaving. The room became "empty" is the only way to describe it, and I knew I was alone, all alone. I'd heard doctors and nurses report this same strange thing happening to them at the moment of death of a patient, but this is the first time it has happened to me. I'm sure that Edna, whom I found out later had been his wife, and Robert, an old friend, long gone, and a lot of others from the way they crowded in, had come for Walter, to take him across into their life. It wasn't frightening, really. I felt comfortable, and hope that when my time comes, some of my friends will come for me so I won't feel lonely and scared of the new adventure of going to the other side."

My daughter, Patricia, now a Marine Corps nurse, before entering the corps, worked for a while in the Cedars Of Lebanon Hospital Intensive Care Ward, in Los Angeles. Without ever having heard this particular phenomenon from me, she came home one night from the hospital and in wide-eyed wonder, related practically the same thing happening to her; the room filling up with presences, the patient expiring, the room "clearing out." It isn't an uncommon occurence and gives added testimony to the fact that we aren't as alone here on earth as we sometimes think we are, like it or not!

Just Checkin' Pardner

This telekinetic, clairaudient story was told me on November 4, 1969, and comes from a long-time friend, Benno Huene, who has lived in Bridgeport, California, for about fifteen years. Benno presently owns a commercial marina on fish-full Bridgeport Lake, rents boats, sells sporting goods, and owns an airplane which he and his wife, affectionately called Butch, use to fly to Rio Valarta, Mexico, where they spend the winters in a trailer court they also own.

The place where this phenomenon took place is Monoville, California, one of the ghost towns that no longer physically exists in Mono County. Springing into being at an elevation of 7,800 feet, it was about ten miles from Bridgeport and was famous for its stream-bed placer gold mining at one time. Monoville almost became the county seat, but the gold ran out and so did the few thousand residents.

In 1873, there were two gold miners up Monoville way, whom we shall call Jack and Dolar. They worked a placer claim on a nearby creek. They had dug a shaft down about forty feet, to bedrock, and had produced quite a good-sized sack of gold. Their bank was a hole in the little hill out behind their tent; they kept the gold, claim papers, and personal letters in a metal box.

One day while they were working down in the shaft, Jack had to come to the surface to get some tools. After he'd selected what they needed, he headed back toward the shaft. Suddenly he heard a rumbling from within the hole, a cloud of dust whooshed up into the air. Running over, he looked down into their shaft. It had caved in! Was half-full of earth and rock. They had not timbered it strongly enough, and stream gravel is notorious for not having the adhesive earthy property to keep it from collapsing. Earth, on the other hand, that hasn't been previously disturbed or penetrated, is stable, but still has to be timbered, or should be, if it is tunneled. Digging would have been useless at this point. The shaft dropped straight down, and now it had at least twenty feet of debris in it, covering his partner, Dolar.

Other nearby miners were hastily called, and all concurred about not being able to get to Dolar in time to save him, there was nothing protective at the bottom of the shaft under which Dolar could have hidden. They were all sure he was already dead. Digging him out would have taken the better part of a day. So, they filled in the shaft to the top and placed a marker on it, giving Dolar's name, birthday, and date of his death.

Jack, after a period of mourning for friend Dolar, began to dig another shaft nearby, using the same tent as his headquarters, and putting the gold into the same cache. No other person knew of his hiding place.

About two weeks after Dolar's untimely death, Jack opened the metal box to put more gold dust into the sack. He noticed that the papers, particularly Dolar's papers, had been disturbed. They were folded differently. You know how you fold some papers a certain way, your own way, when you put them away. Actually, the whole cache had been rummaged through. Nothing was missing, just moved about out of its accustomed place. Dolar's papers had been undoubtedly unfolded, refolded, and placed back in the cannister. Jack didn't pay much attention to it, thinking perhaps he'd done it himself. As the weeks went by and he reopened the cannister to place more gold dust or nuggets in it, he would find that the papers and the gold sack had been disturbed again; the papers not folded the way he had left them, the string securing the gold sack undone.

Then he began placing things in a manner only he would recognize, only to find them moved. Letters on top of the pile would be at the bottom, the gold pouch moved from the left side of the cannister to the right side. One morning, going out to check the cache, he found four letters in a little packet tied with a string. They were addressed to Dolar, and had always been in the metal box, but there they were, lying on the little trail from the tent to the cache, in full view. The gold had not been disturbed, the ground was in the same condition Jack had left it the last time he got into it.

The new shaft didn't prove lucrative enough, and Jack scouted about for another location. One day, months after Dolar's death, Jack was walking up the stream bed wondering where in the world to start another shaft. He told later that he "heard" a voice distinctly say, "Jack, dig over there, to your left." He stood there for some moments waiting to see if he would hear more. Not another physical soul but himself was in the area. He walked to the stream bank, to the left, the direction he'd been "told." Upon reaching the bank, he stopped. Then the voice said, "Right here." Subsequently he did dig there and hit an extremely rich pocket of placer, down at bedrock, which enabled him to sell out and retire to Bodie, California, where he bought some property and spent his declining years. Jack is buried in the cemetery at Bodie.

To the end of his life, Jack swore by all that's holy, he heard Dolar tell him where to dig, and that it was definitely Dolar's voice.

Perhaps if Jack had known about automatic writing, he could have received messages that way from Dolar. When it is suggested to some people, by astrologers and mediums that they try automatic writing, their astrological chart has shown occult propensities or the medium perhaps "heard" that the sitter could communicate that way. When ministers suggest that we "listen for the small voice," I think they mean clairaudience.

The Old Lady
of the Hallway
and the Knocking Ghost

Three disastrous fires in what is now the old ghost town of
Bodie, California, ruined the town and drove away most of
the populace. The last fire levelled the house this story is
concerned with.

Principal among the inhabitants in that mining town's hey-
day was the Cain family. During the 1880s, Mr. Cain, Sr., was
the local banker in Bodie, and lived with his family in a two-
story rented house. After the second fire, the family moved
to Bridgeport, about twenty-six miles away. They became
prominent there, too. In 1946 I met a son, David V. Cain, Jr.,
whose Mother, Ella M. Cain, recently deceased, wrote extensively of the life and times of Bodie; her book, *The Story
Of Bodie,* is currently in publication.

David Cain, called "Vicky" by most everybody, relates
that he was born in Bodie and lived there for many years. His
first recollection of "the old lady of the hallway" goes back
to when he was seventeen. He'd been out of town attending
boarding school, and upon return to his family, he inquired
the whereabouts of the Chinese man they employed to do
housework and who had lived in the house, sleeping in a
small room curtained off from the upstairs hallway.

The family told him the man had come downstairs on

three different occasions and said that during the night some "woman" standing in the hallway, would part the curtains to the room where he was sleeping, wake him up, then just stand there looking at him. He tried to talk to her but she never answered. After the third visit by her he quit and moved out!

A couple of years after that, Vicky and a boy friend, his same age, attended a dance in Bodie during school vacation at the Miners Union Hall, then went to the Cain home to spend the night. The family had moved by this time but the two beds in the small curtained-off room upstairs still remained. The two went to bed in that room. Vicky didn't remember how long he'd been asleep when his friend awakened him to report that he'd been disturbed by the curtains hitting him in the face. He was sleeping in the bed nearest the hall. When he looked up at the curtains, he saw "some old woman, in a shawl, holding the curtains back, just standing there in the hall looking at me!" He said he could see her quite plainly as the moon was coming in the window and shining right on the drapes. This scared Vicky, who immediately remembered the story of the Chinese houseboy.

After telling his friend about the first visitations, that the woman was a ghost, Vicky said he had to really move fast to dress and get out of the house at the same time his friend did. The friend said later that the woman was dressed in clothes like they wore in Bodie in the early days, and that she was what he would call an elderly woman, wrinkled. As Vicky concluded: "That was thirty-three years ago, but I've never forgotten the old lady of the hallway. I wonder if she continued to hang around there after the house burned to the ground?"

"The Knocking Ghost" is the second story Vicky had

which happened in the same house prior to the ghost of the old woman appearing. This experience took place, as he says, thirty-five years ago.

One afternoon while the family were sitting in the downstairs living room there were three loud knocks on the wall of the room. Vicky got up and answered the door but no one was there. Mr. Cain came to the door, also, stepped outside and looked around. No one was near.

Two days later they received word a relative had died in Bridgeport. They didn't associate the knocks they'd heard with the death until some weeks later when they again heard the same three, measured knocks somewhere in the house. Again there was no one at the door, nor near the house. Two days later a friend of theirs died in Bodie.

The family took counsel and decided there was something to the knocks, as though someone was letting them know a relative or friend was going to die. The following month, the same three knocks were heard. The family was greatly upset, fearful of the news they just knew they would receive within a couple of days.

This time a neighbor was thrown from his horse, landed on his head, and was dead before 10 P.M. of the second day!

After that, and until they finally moved to Bridgeport, there were no more knocks . . . as Vicky said, "Thank goodness." The spirit who had been keeping track on who was going to die next, must have decided to move on.

From the foregoing case of "The Knocking Ghost" of the Cain family, we again can see that souls on the "other side," in lieu of materialization, will cause sounds to be made which they know will attract the attention of the proper party, and communicate a message or a warning.

How sounds are produced phantasmally has not, as yet, been explained, but that it is done there is no doubt . . . done for reasons we still have to decipher. At some seances the communicators have asked the excarnate spirit to spell out messages by the use of knocks, raps, or by table tilting; and it has been done under the strictest conditions, in full light. Those messages have been fragmentary, consisting mostly of yes or no answers to questions. Some excarnates and researchers on this side have worked out a morse code type communication whereby they tap or knock out rather long messages.

The best means of communication for the majority of us is automatic writing, though we might wish the channels were more clear and direct.

Through the physical mediumship of such renowned sensitives as Arthur Ford of Florida, Ena Twigg of England, and George Daisley of Santa Barbara, California, voluminous recorded and authenticated direct evidence has been compiled.

As far as receiving help, in the sense of solving our daily or personal problems, Mr. Ford has partially explained the lack of it this way: "It has been proven by many psychiatrists and psychologists, that if a child is given too much help, everything smoothed over for them, the problem solved by doting parents, relatives or friends; the child just naturally won't strive hard enough to solve its problems for itself, although it has the ability to do so. I feel, through what has been received by my mediumship, from my control, Fletcher, those on the other side are really not allowed to solve our earthly problems for us, much as they would like to." (For more on Fletcher, see *Nothing So Strange,* or *Unknown But Known.* both by Arthur Ford.)

We are here to progress by ourselves, not to have it done

for us. At times we do receive subliminal uprushes of knowledge we cannot account for and which can clarify something knotty we've been working on. Artists, writers, and businessmen report this quite frequently. Their answers come usually after they have tried to work a problem out, then relaxed, put it aside, and perhaps slept. In some cases they've had a direct voice speak to them and give them the answer. What is given is enough to whet our appetite to continue the search for the answer to the phenomenon.

Bird
of Ill Omen

Now that we have been on the subject of Knocking Ghosts, let's explore the same phenomenon of a feathered friend accomplishing the same end result. Grace Brandon and John Sturgeon are sister and brother. They live in Bridgeport, California. Grace admits to being some eight years younger than John, who is eighty-four. The interesting astrological aspect of these two is they were born on the exact same day, eight years apart, on September 23. Astrologically, this indicates the two have a karmic tie *(karmic,* the specifics: each individual act, good or bad, will be debted or rewarded—sometimes immediately, sometimes in the future life or lives, but always it will be paid), and it could very well hold true in this particular case. John is somewhat severely crippled. He gets around, but his hips and legs cause him much difficulty. Grace has now devoted her life to caring for him, when it would be just as easy for her to let him be carted off to an old folk's home which are now called convalariums.

At the time of the phenomena, the Sturgeon family lived in Bodie, but their house was not right in the center of town, rather it was on the road to the other now ghost town of Aurora, a few miles north of Bodie.

One day she and her mother were cleaning house, when their attention was attracted by something knocking at the window. Grace walked over and pulled back the curtain. A large, black bird was bumping up against it, striking the glass and fluttering. It hit so hard one time that it fell to the ground, stunned. Grace ran outside and knelt down beside it. When it had sufficiently come to, it flew up again, and continued bumping into the glass pane, bump, bump, bump.

It did this for about a minute, then it flew away. When Grace went back inside, her mother was sitting at the dining table, looking very white and disturbed. Mrs. Sturgeon told her that she'd seen the same thing happen before.

A bird would flutter and bump against a window, and within a short time, word would arrive that some friend, or relative, had died.

No news of any portent arrived for the Sturgeons for some time. Mail was slow in getting up to Bodie in the old days. Within a month, Mrs. Sturgeon received word from a friend in Los Angeles that a very close friend of theirs had died. They checked the date of the day the bird had beat against the window and which Mrs. Sturgeon had noted on her calendar. The friend had died on the day the bird brought the message.

Coincidence? Hmmmm.

This particular phenomenon isn't unknown by any means. The same occurrence has been reported over the years many times. I have read about it when I was a boy in Illinois, of it happening locally. The interesting question which comes to mind is, How is the word transmitted to one of our feathered friends about where they are to go to deliver that message?

A Voice
from the Past

Charley Otto, a friend of mine, called me from the club recently and said he'd heard I was doing a book on ghosts and strange unexplainable phenomenon and asked if I needed some more material, which, of course, I assured him was the case—my interest in ghostly phenomena extends much farther than just a book! His father had told the story many times, and although he didn't know whether it would fit in with what I was doing, he wanted to hear it again himself.

When the father, Harry, was a young man, he drove a twenty-mule team for the Borax works in Death Valley, California. The year was 1889. As Harry and his new partner were driving the loaded wagon out of the valley one day, they noticed the entrance to a mine tunnel up on the side of a hill beside the narrow dirt road. The day was exceedingly hot, as only midsummer days can get in that most desolate of desert areas, like 125 degrees. They stopped the team, climbed down, took their canteens, and proceeded to climb the hill to the tunnel, if for nothing more than to get out of the heat for awhile.

They entered the tunnel and walked perhaps fifty feet when Harry heard his name called out, loud and clear. He turned to his friend, who said, "Did you hear that?" Harry said he'd heard it, that someone, and it sounded like a former partner who used to drive with him, was calling him. The man had been killed two years ago. They agreed the voice sounded as though it was coming from outside the tunnel so they made their way back to the opening, stepped out and looked around. No one was there. They stood for a few moments, very puzzled. Harry knew it hadn't been an hallucination; he alone hadn't heard things because his partner had heard the voice too; it had repeated his name twice. There was no explanation for it, and Harry did possibly think they'd both imagined it, which his partner hotly denied. They discussed it for awhile, then decided to go back in and see if it would happen again, thinking that perhaps it had been caused by a breeze blowing over something in the tunnel. They reentered the tunnel and walked back to approximately where they had been when they heard the voice.

The voice came again, calling Harry by name, and there was no doubt about it. This time it was imperative, demanding, like a military order: "Harry, Harry, come out, now." They both moved much faster than usual to reach the entrance, step out, and demanded loudly for the person calling to show themself.

In that moment, as they were standing some five feet outside the tunnel, there was that sickening crunch. It seemed the whole tunnel collapsed at once, the first ten feet of the overburden immediately over the entrance going first ... plunk.

Harry and his partner hung around for another half hour trying their best to communicate with "the voice" of Harry's deceased friend, then drove the wagon on into the desert town of Mojave to relate the story to the fellows at the railhead where they dumped off the borax.

During many trips after that, Harry would stop off at the collapsed mine tunnel and walk around the whole area, calling aloud for his excarnate friend. There was never another communication from "the other side," which is what both men were convinced they'd heard; and there was never a doubt that the ex-earthling had been with them on that trip, knew of the impending disaster, and warned them in time to save their lives.

Clairaudience is not unusual, and many thousands of incidences have been recorded, but they are certainly unusual to the individual or individuals to whom they occur.

Remember when you thought you heard a voice, and no one was present? You, no doubt, did hear it! It wasn't a figment of your imagination.

"We Like
Our Ghost"

This business of hunting up ghost stories is probably like any other human endeavor. There are good days and bad, full periods and lax. The present period is most satisfyingly full. But, did you ever think you'd finished a job, then find it only half done? Admittedly, this is the most fascinating job I've ever undertaken, so it will be a pleasure to continue unearthing stories.

On the evening of April 2, 1970, I arrived at the home of Dick and Lavonne Atwood, on Petit Street, Granada Hills, California, hopefully to secure what purported to be a good story. For one and a half hours I sat completely absorbed in possibly the most fascinating discourse on poltergeistic phenomena it's been my extreme pleasure to encounter, so far.

The four Atwood children were in bed, but infrequently, one of them would wander into the front room where we were sitting, wanting a drink, or whatever. For the poltergeist researcher, I will add that all the children are under the age of fifteen; the Atwoods have been investigated by a member of the Southern California Society For Psychical Research (SCSPR), and a member of the Duke University Parapsychology Research Department, jointly. Their stamp of authenticity has been placed on them as having "ghostly" manifestations, true psychic phenomena. This is the first time it's been written up.

The Atwoods bought the house new, five years ago. About six months after they moved in, each, separately, noticed strange happenings. Dick Atwood would "see" a cloud of mist floating down the hall. Once he saw a blue light. Lavonne saw a blue light from time to time. The light was about four or five inches in height, like a blue flame. It didn't emit any sparks or diffusion as though it was an electrical charge, just a blue flame. Neither of them spoke to the other about what they'd seen, thinking they would be laughed at, or, even worse, that perhaps there *was* something there!

One night Dick was sitting watching television after putting the children to bed. All of a sudden, out of the corner of his eye, he saw "someone" walk into the kitchen, and he got up to go see who it was. When he walked into the kitchen area, no one was there but himself. After this had happened on two or three more occasions, he broke down and told Lavonne. She then admitted she'd been seeing something much the same, and they began to compare notes.

Dick sort of figured it must be some kind of light reflection that was causing the flame or ball of mist. Pulling down the blinds did no good. They got a bunch of army blankets and hung them over all the windows in the kitchen and living room, but still the blue flame would appear, sometimes the mist. Dick sees the manifestation more often as the mist; Lavonne sees the blue flame, infrequently the mist. Originally the mist or flame would go by quite rapidly, its presence would be noted sort of out of the corner of your eye, but you knew you'd seen "it."

They had a German shepherd and a cat at the time, and when either the flame or the mist was present, moving up the hall from the direction of the bedrooms and into the kitchen area, the dog would growl, its hackles standing straight up; the cat would, as they said, "fizz up." The dog slunk to the corner of the hallway one night as though tracking or stalking something, and the cat followed him, all fizzed up. Sure enough, the flame emerged from the hall, made its usual way into the kitchen. Sometimes the flame turns and instead of going into the kitchen, exits the house through the door, without opening it, of course. One night the flame emerged from the hallway, and the cat leaped straight up in the air about two feet as cats sometimes do when they are surprised by something.

The flame or mist has always been observed coming from the direction of the bedroom or bathroom, both of which are at the north end of the house. It then moves south down the hall, emerges from the hall, crosses the front door entry and enters the kitchen, and, as I said, sometimes turns after coming out of the hall and goes out through the closed front door. A few times it has turned left, gone into the front room.

Once it positioned itself near the divider shutters which separate the front room from the kitchen, just off to the left of the chair in which Dick Atwood was sitting. Dick said he finally saw it, and he watched it for about fifteen minutes; then, when he started to get up, it went out, or wherever. Lavonne saw it at the same time and got up, went around behind the shutters to see if she could still see the light from the other side of the shutters. She couldn't. It was only visible when standing directly "in front" of it.

During these first manifestations, Lavonne, who suffers from insomnia, was sitting in the front room about 2:30 A.M. She was sitting in a chair in the southeast corner of the room, with a floor lamp behind her right shoulder. Suddenly she "felt" someone was in the room with her, and she thought it was Dick. She didn't look completely up, more like at an angle at the floor, out about ten feet from her chair. She saw a pair of old, dirty boots, and some kind of homespun billowy pants, poked into the tops of the boots. The boots were black, the pants dark brown. It surprised her so much she gave an involuntary gasp, and as she did so the apparition went into a puff of mist and disappeared right through the shutters. Lavonne said her hair stood on end, she started shaking, and decided she'd better go to bed, quick. She laid awake until five in the morning, and told Dick all about what had happened.

Lavonne and Dick have communicated with their guest through the Ouija board. They "get on" the board, and whatever it was that moved the planchette, seemed to take over Dick. When Lavonne works the board with someone else, she seems to be the power focus.

Dick works hard at his job with the California National Guard in Van Nuys, and when he comes home at night, eats his dinner, and unless it's Friday night, so he can sleep late on Saturday, goes to bed early. One evening he came home and went straight to bed, but only slept until about 7:30, and when he awakened, said he'd done it on purpose, so he could stay up and try to make contact through the board with whomever was living in the house with them. They were on the board about ten minutes, and Dick became completely exhausted, as if somebody had drained off all his energy. It happened every time Dick and Lavonne communicated through the Ouija board. Within ten minutes Dick would be drained dry. The couple has excellent communication between themselves, but when they try to work the board together, it drains off Dick's vital energy.

During that ten minutes on the board, there is also excellent communication with, and they said the ghost's name for the first time, Noel. Noel Sepulveda, he calls himself, through the Ouija board.

Then I asked a few questions. "Who is he?"

"Well, he says he's the illegitimate son of Don Sepulveda, who, according to the history books, owned the land where our house is. Sepulveda, California, is named after the Sepulveda family. His mother's name was April Christian. She was an English bond servant who came over on the boat with the people who settled here, and Don Sepulveda had her as his mistress, on this property.

"The reason Noel says he will never leave the land is because he promised his mother just before her death that he would never leave his inheritance, and he's given us to believe that his inheritance was this land, and nothing else. He says he will always be in this house, as long as it is here."

"He hasn't tried to oust you from here, has he?"

"Oh, no, in fact, he's actually saved our lives. I firmly believe it."

The deeper we got, the better it became, and they seemed to be having so much good, excited interest, I kept my questions on the light side. There was much laughter and good-natured banter throughout the entire session with the Atwoods.

"Ok, so he saved your lives. How?"

"Right. Ok, well, it was cold and windy this one night, and we'd been out to a party, and we'd left all the windows open in the house. When we came in it was just freezing, so we went around, shutting all the windows, told the kids to go to bed, and we turned the heat way up, to like eighty-five or ninety.

We went to bed, and we were real tired, and we forgot to lower the heat or open the windows after the house had gotten warm. I don't know how much later it was when Dick all of a sudden jumped up and said, 'What do you want?' And I said, 'What, what did you say?' Then I noticed that it was almost like a blast furnace in the room; it was *hot;* we were covered with perspiration. We went in and got the kids up, and they were like they were drugged. We opened the windows. lowered the furnace and cooled the place off a bit.

After all this excitement, we got the kids back to bed, went into the kitchen and had a cup of coffee, and relaxed a little bit. Dick said, 'Boy, it's a good thing you woke me up.' I said I hadn't done anything. He said that somebody sure did!"

Lavonne turned to Dick, and asked him to tell it like it happened to him.

"Well, somebody yelled 'Dick,' real loud, right in my ear. I sat up and said 'What do you want?' I figured it was Lavonne. Then, one night he woke my wife up by yelling in her ear. She decided to check the kids, and our daughter was running a temperature of 102 degrees. If she hadn't gotten up we could have had a nasty situation on our hands."

I had to ask, "Lavonne, how did he awaken you, what did he say?"

"This time I heard his voice. It wasn't a real deep voice, but it was a man's voice. And it said, 'Lavonne, get up quick.' It woke me up in an instant, and I knew it was Noel then, and I got up, and sure enough, Kathie was just burning up.

She was red as a beet, and I grabbed the bottle of alcohol and rubbed her all over until the fever went down. And you know, the children have seen him."

I didn't want to break her train of thought so I just sat quietly, expectantly. She continued. "The two younger ones have actually seen him, in full view."

Then I couldn't help asking, "How about the two older ones, have they seen him?" "No, the two older ones haven't seen him at all."

We stopped here for a moment to discuss the reasons why some people can see apparitions and some can't. It is generally accepted that the more psychic an individual is, the more likely he'll see apparitions. It is interesting that the older ones have not even seen the "light" which heralds the presence of Noel.

Dick picked up the conversation. "As far as the younger children, first it was Kathie. She wet her bed one night, and I told her she was getting too old to wet the bed anymore and asked why she didn't go to the bathroom? She said she did get up to go to the bathroom, but he wouldn't let her pass. I asked her who wouldn't let her pass, and she started describing this man who was standing right next to the bathroom door, in the hallway. We thought she was a little too young to tell her about ghosts so we just let it go at that. About a week later, Timothy wet his bed, and it was the same story. We hadn't, either one of us, talked to the other children about it. We had talked to them separately, and didn't tell them it was a ghost. Timothy came up with almost the identical description Kathie had; this man was standing in the hallway and wouldn't let him pass."

In all my years of reading and discussing the occult, ghosts, etc., I've only heard of a few instances of actual physical contact, but when it happens, it can be quite rude. Dick Atwood went into this next one. "One night he slapped me. I thought it was my wife, and I was ready to roll over and belt her a good one." "Were you asleep, Dick?"

"Oh, yeah. Noel came into the bedroom and slapped me. When I turned over, Lavonne was laying with her back to me, and to slap me she would have dislocated her arm, in the position she was in. And she was asleep."

Lavonne gave a delighted laugh at this. Then she picked it up.

"That night, Dick had been teasing me, unmercifully, and I told him, I said, 'Oh, I could just slap you one, but I'm just too much of a lady.' "

They didn't remember that ghosts have big ears!

"I said to Dick I should get Noel to really clobber you, and he said, 'Sure, sure, you and your boy friend,' just like that. And then we went to bed, and POW, he got it. Apparently Noel sided with me and decided to whack his face."

More questions kept popping up which I had to ask from time to time. "Do the kids know what he looks like? How did they describe him?"

Lavonne said, "They described him as a medium-tall man, they said about grandpa's size. Well, my dad is five-foot-ten, and they said that the man had on old clothes, and they were all dark color, greys and browns, and he had on boots. The most interesting thing about it—and first we were worried about it—neither one of the kids were afraid of it all. In fact, if anything, they sort of got a big kick out of it. They sounded very put out that he wouldn't let them in the bathroom, and said, 'Oh, he wouldn't let us pass,' disgusted rather than scared, like they were talking about one of the brothers. I told them that next time they should ask him to please move, and they said all right. You know how kids wake up; they are sort of groggy. Well, the next morning after it had happened, they didn't remember all that they had told me, because I asked them about what happened. It's really wild, isn't it?"

One day Lavonne was giving Kathie a bath. A glass was sitting on the sink behind her, and in moving around she knocked it over into the sink, and it broke, with a loud noise. Dick, who was in the other room, came running down the hall, and ran right through the cloud of mist he knew to be Noel Sepulveda! For some reason, Noel was moving in the other direction—out. There was no collision; Dick just passed right through it. I asked him if there had been any feeling of coldness, clamminess? He said, no, he just passed right through it. There wasn't any feeling, except he knew he'd gone through the ghost. He stopped and looked back, and the cloud went on down the hall and turned the corner as if going out the door.

Usually, when someone has had a contact experience with a ghost, they have reported the cold feeling, a clamminess, but not this time. And Noel was quite solid when he slapped Dick. As Dick said, going through Sepulveda *startled* him more than anything else. They recounted this incident to Mr. Bayless of Duke University Psychology team, and Mr. Hendrickson of the SCSPR, when they were investigating.

On that same occasion, Mr. Bayless was sitting in the hallway. There were thirteen people present in the house at the time (fourteen counting Noel, to stay away from that unlucky number!). All of a sudden, a window in the bathroom went up about a foot. The door was open, so Mr. Bayless could see either down the hall or into the bathroom, and then he watched it close. There was no one there, in physical form. It just opened and closed by itself (not *really* if Noel did it).

That same night, as Dick told it, the large table lamp I was sitting next to audibly snapped off on two separate occasions. He thought it could be the cat playing with the cord, but he noticed that one of the kids had the cat on his lap in the kitchen. He jerked the cord, hit the lamp, snapped it on and off, then left it off and stepped away from it. In a few moments it snapped back on again. That was in the presence of the thirteen people.

For the astrologers, Lavonne was born August 5, 1931, in Los Angeles, at about five o'clock in the morning. Dick was born June 8, 1929, Minneapolis, Minnesota, about three o'clock in the morning. That should provide the buff with enough to ascertain if either of the Atwoods are psychic, and to what extent. I should have gotten the birth data on the Atwood children, but I didn't. It is believed by some researchers that when a ghost is present, look to the youngsters in the house. When most parapsychologists first learn of a case of alleged paranormal displacement of objects, particularly, the first question is likely to be, "Are there any adolescents in the house?" Usually it has been found there is at least one present. That child could be undergoing severe mental or emotional problems, and in some manner this state is transferred to things, objects, outside the child, and can manifest in psychokinesis (PK), movement of objects by some unknown mind-directed energy. Usually the person starting all this PK isn't even aware of it.

Objects have not been observed flying about the Atwood house or penetrating anything. This seems to be just what it is purported to be, the continuing life of Noel Sepulveda, illegitimate son of Don Sepulveda and April Christian. I am wondering how the experts square with their definition of ghost as "a material being without a physical occupant" in this case? Did you ever get slapped by a blue flame or a cloud of mist?

The Atwoods think perhaps Noel "lives" in the wall furnace! In the summer they turn off the pilot light; there is no heat or activity within the heater, as they don't use it for air-conditioning. They've walked past the furnace and heard a rhythmic thump-thump, thump, thump. Frequently they hear high-pitched music, muted, coming from the furnace. Occasionally they've heard people talking, far away, in tiny voices—nothing distinguishable. I wonder if Noel has a family in there? What happens when the family grows up? Will the Atwoods have a whole housefull of Sepulveda ghosts?

One night a cousin of Lavonne's was over, and the group went to the Ouija board. Lavonne asked the board if it had any message for Jean? It did: "Be very careful of your door."

Jean got very excited because they were having trouble with their car door and were afraid it would come open while they were driving. That was just a week before my meeting with the Atwoods.

Two friends, George and Mary Martin, came over one night, and they had a Ouija board session. Noel would come through with messages for Mary, but not for George. George got all shook up—plumb rejected. Noel did appear twice as the blue flame, in the room, but he wouldn't talk to George. George demanded he be allowed to sit at the board, ordered Noel to give him a message. Lavonne worked the board with him. She asked Noel if he couldn't bring a message for George? One word was spelled out—*Humbug*. Apparently this is George's favorite word when he doesn't believe something. His wife, Mary, knew he used it, but the Atwoods didn't.

Mary got back on the board with Lavonne, and it wouldn't answer any questions, but seemed quite excited, the planchette travelling quickly all over the board. Finally it did spell out *Ed, go, check Ed.* The planchette moved very sharply. Many times it is difficult to know which letter the pointer is actually indicating, but this time there was no doubt. They all went into the bedroom, and young Ed was sleeping with his mouth open, snoring quite loudly! Noel didn't like snoring, it disturbed him. When they returned to the board, it wrote out one word—*Good.* After that, Noel was more tractable, except for ignoring George, and answered most questions they put to him.

Noel has said he is a young man, about thirty-five years of age. Says he is *muy simpatico;* he keeps telling the Atwoods not to be afraid. Noel comes through the board in both Spanish and English, mixing the two. Lavonne has a Spanish background, but, as her grandmother told her many years ago, "Just talk English, you ruin the language with your American accent, and your father's Russian." And they've never spoken Spanish since Lavonne was a little girl.

Mr. Bayless, from Duke University, said he was a ghost writer, probably meaning he could do automatic writing. He positioned himself in the hallway with a pad of legal paper, and allowed Noel to enter his body, as he put it, take over his hand and do some writing. Bayless said he doesn't know Spanish at all, and he got very excited at what was coming through. In the writings, Noel said, "I am here, make sure I am here." Then there was some reference to a General Ybarra, *muerto,* i.e., "General Ybarra, dead."

Many years ago, during the early 1800s, the era of Don Sepulveda and his son Noel, there was a General Ybarra, and to this day there is doubt and controversy over just exactly where the General is buried. They didn't know this at the time of the writings, but I've asked the Atwoods to try and find out where the general is really buried, put the record to bed. It's in San Fernando Valley, somewhere. It was also during Mr. Bayless' period of automatic writing that the window in the bathroom opened and closed, which Mr. Bayless observed, and was properly impressed.

My misfortune was that only the previous night Noel had appeared about half a dozen times. During the time I was in the Atwood house, he didn't show up once. I've left a standing request that anytime he begins appearing, I would appreciate a call, and I would get there within a few minutes!

When the investigators first called Lavonne about coming out for a look-see, she told them they were welcome, that she and Dick had nothing to hide. They know Noel is there. They have him! Of course, as we know, that night Noel really put on a show. The two investigators, to repeat, did say that, yes, the Atwoods did have a paranormal manifestation. They didn't know how it occurred except they had observed it.

Interestingly too, it has been noted that at times ghosts will frequent a place for some time; then—nothing for perhaps a week up to a couple of months, then the activity begins again. It was explained by Mr. Bayless that ghosts, like us, have to take a vacation once in a while, rejuvenate themselves, get a change of locale. After all, they are much like we are.

Regarding Mr. Hendrickson, from the Southern California Society For Psychical Research, Lavonne told me he was a very nice man, but that Noel didn't like him! Didn't want him in the house, would have nothing to do with him. Noel was not *muy simpatico* with Mr. Hendrickson. After that session there was a two-week hiatus period when Noel was absent from the Ouija board sittings, and his blue flame or mist didn't show. Then, when he did manifest again, he made it quite plain he didn't like the man, and did not want them to have him over again. Lavonne called Mr. Hendrickson, told him how Noel felt. The gentleman, knowing ghosts (or any people, for that matter), was very understanding, said that it happens sometimes, ghosts not wanting to talk to certain people. Ghosts are just as "human" as we are, they have their likes and dislikes, too. Noel actually punished the Atwoods by not showing up for them. He was sulking.

They also asked Noel, through the Ouija board, if there was any buried treasure? His answer was that it was buried under the oak tree. The trouble is, there isn't any oak tree! They've all been removed to make room for all the homes being built. Which oak tree, where? I think he was indulging another of his games with them.

Noel hasn't been able to materialize, but both Dick and Lavonne feel he will one day. Particularly in the morning, when Lavonne is putting on makeup in the dressing room, she has had a distinct feeling of a presence, almost like the warmth from a close human body, heard subdued breathing.

Now we come to the part which Dick has a rather difficult time with. It seems that in her dreams, Lavonne "steps out." She has no memory where she has been, but when she awakens she feels as though she's been to a party, talked with a great many people, been places. She told me that after one of those dreams she felt wonderful, all day. Dick didn't look too happy when she was relating this. Can't say I blame him. What all does go on during those astral parties?

It is known that most of us do leave our bodies when we are asleep, and do some traveling. Some call it recharging their batteries. The physical body needs physical rest, the astral body needs spirit rest. The question that comes to mind is, what happens when you run into some of your dirty little friends out there? Dick gave a nasty laugh, and I could see he would have a few words with Lavonne after I'd left, like, "You don't have to bring that out-of-body travel in, it could be misunderstood!"

Lavonne has a first cousin, Dolly, who is a Pisces, is psychic, and when she learned about Noel, nothing would do but she pay the Atwoods a visit, *pronto*. She wanted to see if she could communicate with him, with their ghost, as she put it. Dolly is also a trance-medium, and has both a Spanish and a Hindu spirit she is in contact with. As heretofore mentioned, neither the Atwoods nor Dolly speak anything but a very broken Spanish.

When Dolly arrived, in the afternoon, she went immediately into the kitchen, seated herself at the table and went into trance, after telling them to converse with whomever came through, and let her know who it was, what was said. Her Spanish was perfect! Castilian. Her voice became very deep and low-pitched, and suddenly this beautiful laughter came out of her. The voice identified itself as Noel! Supposedly (unless Dolly is a fantastic actress), Noel repeated the same things he'd told them previously, and added that he'd died of smallpox, but didn't show the scars anymore.

Noel addressed Lavonne and Dick personally to the effect that he did want to appear to them, that he would when the conditions were proper. They asked what the proper conditions were, if they could help out, but got no answer. Some trade secrets I guess we just couldn't divulge. He added that he was glad they were pleased he lived in their house, on his land(!), that he tried not to make things unpleasant for them, and liked to see a family as happy as they all were. With that he bid them *buenas tardes* and went off the air. When they told Dolly what had been said, how she used perfect Castilian, talked in Noel's voice, she was ecstatic. She couldn't remain any longer, but promised to return, and I added when the story was finished that if I couldn't get in on the next sitting, I would be most unhappy. This is better than TV or movies, any ghostly day!

The last item the Atwoods regaled me with, concerned a guest they entertained one evening. A man and his wife. The man, according to Lavonne, was over sixty, but looked much older, his face quite lined and wrinkled. He walked like a much older man, flat-footed, lifeless. During the evening he had occasion to visit the bathroom, and excused himself. Some few minutes later they heard laughter from the hallway. Everyone crowded into the hall, hoping Noel hadn't scared the man. To the contrary, that "old" man had undergone a transformation! He was cutting a dance step, his face had become almost young again, unlined, his eyes were bright and sparkling. He said it was the greatest feeling he'd had since he was a young man, and wanted to dance with Lavonne. They were afraid to let him do too much because he did have a bad heart, and the exertion might do him in.

After persuading him to return to the front room, he took his seat in the armchair, and it wasn't long before he again became the man he'd been prior to encountering Noel in the hallway. Somehow Noel had pumped life and vitality into him. The man kept saying he wanted more of that hallway, but they didn't let him return. Who knows, maybe Noel wanted some new company on the other side? I can't think harshly of such a nice, considerate ghost. Perhaps he doesn't think getting out of our physical husks is so bad.

It is only our own fear of the unknown which really bugs

us about departing terra firma. Some of the communicating ghosts have made the other side sound very attractive, not something to fear. They say it's the same, but different, so different they can't explain it, or so same they can't describe it. That old saying "Everybody wants to go to heaven, nobody wants to die," is so true of most all of us. Of course, in each individual astrological chart there is a moment of birth, and the moment and manner of death, and barring wars, or suicide (which also shows), most of us live out our allotted time span.

The Fountain of Youth hasn't been found, perhaps never will be the way man looks round about and outside himself for it. I believe the Fountain of Youth is within, in the spirit concept of continuing life. There is no death but that of the physical body, and by the time I'm through with mine, I will probably be well satisfied to bid it, "*Adieu, adieu* old friend, *adieu;* I can no longer stay with you. . . .''

"It's a Man in a Cape"

In April of 1969, Mrs. Evelyn Garrett was driving on a street in Studio City, California, in the rain. She suddenly heard —thought a voice which told her to "Slow down, Evelyn." Usually I've found that people don't listen too well when they have these premonitory voices, but this time she paid attention, she's heard the voice before.

She actually pulled over to one side and slowed down. Then the car began to feel as though it was running on the rims, rough, bumpy. Evelyn immediately applied the brake, and the car spun on the slick street, turned almost completely around, and came to rest against a chain-link fence. Naturally, she opened the door and started to get out, and to her astonishment, as she alighted, "someone" got out with her, another entity. (It would have been more astonishing had the "someone," as she got out her door, opened the door on the far side, and they'd both exited! But it didn't happen that way.)

Her first look was at the tires, and *both* rear tires were flat. A woman in a house nearby let her use the phone to call the Automobile Club, and when the attendant was changing the tires, he told her that having two flat tires simultaneously couldn't happen once in half-a-million times, that if she'd been going any faster she would have probably turned over. The tires had been cut or worn through, and just went down. And who was the "other person" who got out of the car with her? It was a shadow figure. It saved her life, then disappeared.

Evelyn's daughter, Diane, took me back to the beginning of their phenomenal story.

The Garretts moved into a house on Riverside Drive, in Studio City, about twenty years ago. It was a brand-new house, no one had occupied it before they moved in. Six weeks after they'd settled in, they heard rattlings, bumpings within the walls, from the attic. At first they laid the noises to the traffic on the street, but it happened when there was no traffic. When the noises continued, Mrs. Garrett finally admitted to Diane and her husband that she'd seen a "figure" in the hall and standing at the foot of her bed. When a person sees, or thinks he sees an apparition, he usually gets scared or at least apprehensive, but Evelyn wasn't. For some reason she wasn't afraid of it.

The figure was said to be wearing a hat and a cape; it was a man. Later, when Diane finally saw it, she understood why her mother had described it in that manner. There was actually no definition. It was about five feet high, a billowy, misty, shadowy "thing," which gave the impression to Diane it could be wearing a hat and a cape, unless as she says, her mother got a clearer picture of it.

One night Diane was lying on her bed reading a book, about 7:30 in the evening. The light was on. She saw, out of the corner of her eye, what she thought was her mother walking through the room in her robe, so she didn't even look up, was just aware. But, when the figure continued walking and disappeared right into the wall, she came to life with a scream at the top of her lungs.

Mrs. Garrett, who was in the living room, of course heard her and came running. Diane was almost incoherent, chattering and gesticulating. Evelyn immediately guessed what had happened, and tried to quiet her. "Calm down, Diane, I've seen it too."

"But mother, it walked right into the wall!"

"I know, I've seen it do that too. He doesn't hurt anyone, he's just here!"

From its size and shape, both women believed it was a man. Mrs. Garrett then admitted she'd been aware of the visitor for some time, she'd seen it often, and was hesitant about telling either her husband or Diane because it really hadn't caused any trouble, bothered anyone. She'd been hoping against hope the other members of the family wouldn't see it. They had no idea who the "man" was.

Diane called the builder and tried to find out if the house was sitting on some kind of burial ground, which it wasn't; there wasn't even a graveyard nearby. Mr. Garrett crawled under the house but could find no nesting place for a possible intruder to hole up.

Other manifestations were the snapping off, or on, of the light switches. Some years later when Diane was dating a young man, the two were in the house one evening when the switches played their games, and the boyfriend almost climbed the wall. Diane tried to explain that they had a "nice" ghost in the house, and I can imagine the boy's probable reaction as he wondered what kind of a coven of witches he'd fallen in with! Diane's physical beauty must have overcome his trepidation; they were later married.

During the next few years, when they would visit her mother, they enquired about the ghost and were told, "Yes, he's been here a few times, he doesn't hurt anyone." They did learn that a friend of Evelyn's, Trudy, had stayed the night, and had awakened to see the apparition standing at the foot of her bed "looking at me!" Evelyn, sleeping in the same room, sat up and said, "That's all right, Trudy, he's a friend of ours," which I'm sure did nothing to allay the hair-raising. Trudy hurriedly arose, dressed, and exited the premises, and she's not been back, although they are still friends—over the phone. Trudy described the *man* as having substance, dark, but you could see through it. He was there.

Astral Projection and Animal Ghosts

Astral
Projection

Astral projection is variously called "out-of-body travel," "bilocation," and "traveling clairvoyance." What does this have to do with anything ghostly? There is a man in Trona, California, who on two different occasions has dreamed he took a trip up a canyon in the Telescope Peak area of the Panamint Valley and found mineral lodes. The dreams were so vivid, he physically made the trip to the spots he saw in his dreams and opened up sizeable enough ore deposits to have sold them at a handsome profit. In Trona, he is looked at askance by some, with reverence by others, envy by some, and placed in the category of being "haunted" by most.

According to some research books on the subject, most of us have experienced astral projection at one time or another, but don't pay too much attention to it, blaming those kookie traveling dreams on something we ate or drank.

There is a story out of Washington, D.C., of a man who approached a department of government and told them he was an astral projector, that he could spy for them outside the country. Someone prevailed upon the nonbelievers to the point they gave it a try. The man was thoroughly checked out officially, didn't have a criminal or mental illness record, and had never been out of the United States. He was told to "visit" the American embassy in London, and when he awakened from his self-induced sleep, draw them a diagram of the embassy office, place all the furniture in the proper places, reveal where our hidden microphones were installed, and let them know if any foreign microphones, or "bugs" were present.

The man was placed in a room, the door locked. He was observed throughout the test through a glass window in the door. He covered his eyes by placing a handkerchief about his head, laid down on a couch provided, and put himself to sleep. In half an hour he awoke, removed the handkerchief, and signaled he was ready to provide the information they'd requested. A draftsman drew in every piece of furniture and detail of the room as the man had seen them on his astral trip. Two hidden microphones in use by our government were correctly placed, and another microphone, of which our side had no knowledge, was included. A call to the embassy in London was made. A few minutes later they reported back that indeed the hitherto unknown microphone had been found where the man "saw" it. Interestingly enough, we are told the Russians are using this same astral technique to spy on us!

My own conscious experience with astral projection is limited to one occurence. I'd been up in Surprise Canyon, in Panamint Valley, California. It is remote, dry, and rugged. On my way out of the canyon, my "trip" took place. The day was cold, but I was warmly dressed. The sun was shining and supplied enough heat to be just comfortable in fairly heavy clothes. The jeep I was using didn't have a top and I'd put the windshield up to break the wind. For a moment I stopped the vehicle on the little path, and just sat there basking. My dog jumped out and began rummaging around to find a lizard to chase. I sank into a kind of dreamy apathy, not awake, not asleep, kind of in between.

Then I felt as though I was rising, lifting, drifting out of my body. It wasn't a disturbing sensation, rather very pleasant. I didn't try to stop what was happening. Finally I seemed to be clear out of the me sitting in the jeep. I could see "me" sitting in the jeep. Then I began to move, as though flying, but it was through no particular motion of my own, without any effort. There was no feeling of cold air blowing against or around me. I don't remember how I was dressed. I gathered speed and covered the valley area which is about twenty-five miles long by five or six miles wide.

For a long time I'd wondered what was at the north end of the valley, but the area was so rough I'd never gotten into it. My trip took me to the far end and I saw the sand dunes, some old diggings of years ago, a few busted-up wagon remains. Then I moved over to the east side, up the slope of the mountain separating Panamint Valley from Death Valley. Down below me I spotted an airplane on the ground. It was wrecked, not totally, but obviously had crashed. No one was visible around the wreckage, the plane's skin looked bright and polished.

Then I moved on, over the canyons on the east side, farther south. My trip seemed to be over because I was again over myself sitting in the jeep, and I began to descend. The free feeling I had was so pleasant I tried my best to keep from going back into me. As I seemed to settle down on me, enter me, again I felt the sun, and sleepily trying to hold onto the experience, stretched—came to. My dog had just returned from whatever he'd been doing, and stood there beside the jeep looking at me. I felt wonderful, and just sat there for a moment remembering what I'd seen . . . the exhiliration.

At dinner that night in the Panamint Springs Motel where I was staying, I told the owners of a crashed airplane and where it was, not going into any detail that I'd been on an astral trip! Only then did I learn that a plane had crashed up there some years ago, the survivors had been taken out by the Forest Service; the engine and the instruments were removed.

Yes, the plane was there and I'd seen it, not from the ground but from the air, and I wasn't in a helicopter or other aircraft when I saw it. Many is the time I've awakened of a morning with the feeling I'd been someplace in my dreams, but this is the only occurrence I can definitely say I took part in and remembered in most every detail. I wrote down the trip upon returning to the motel and used those notes to pass this on.

Two good research books on astral projection are *Projection of the Astral Body,* by Muldoon and Carrington, and *Techniques of Astral Projection,* by Robert Crookall.

"Now You See Me, but You Really Didn't"

Of all the ghostly phenomena encountered, the one which will *absorb* you completely (if I may use that metaphor) is undoubtedly when some living person appears to you someplace other than where they really are, and when you've just seen them on the street in an area or place where you know they shouldn't be, couldn't be, and probably aren't! That sounds confusing, I know, but that's the way it happens.

Pseudonymously, the couple we are talking about are Tim and Carolyn Dickson. They live in San Jose, California, on the east side of town, and that is as exact as they wish their present location to be given. When word of the phenomenal activities got out, there were the usual lunatic fringe who began camping on their doorstep, thinking Tim was a psychic and could put them in touch with friends or relatives on the other side. Of course Tim was also scientifically investigated, and pronounced, if not authentic, at least his manifestation was unexplainable. Tim is the one who exhibits the phenomenon, and Carolyn and some of their friends are merely observers of what occurs with him.

The first time it happened, as Tim told it, he was about sixteen. He was riding his bike, delivering some groceries to a friend of the family who was under the weather. At that time his family lived on the north end of town, and he was making the delivery on the west side. There wasn't anything unusual about the day; it was bright and hot, with a high fog holding some miles away. He completed his delivery, cycled back home, parked the machine, and went into the house.

The first thing his mother asked him was, "Why didn't you deliver the groceries to Mrs. Rocha?" Tim told her he had delivered them, he'd just gotten back. His mother had a strange look on her face, and continued to ask questions. Tim got pretty uncomfortable because it seemed to him he was being accused of lying. What his mother was harping on was that during the time he had supposedly been making the delivery, she had seen him, clearly, riding his bike around the block. She'd seen him pass the house two times. The only way to authenticate the story was to call Mrs. Rocha, which his mother did. She verified that Tim had been where he said he was. There was no explanation for what had occurred, and the consensus of opinion of the family was that there possibly was a new boy in the neighborhood who looked just like Tim, had a bike like his. No new boy was ever found.

This phenomena didn't happen again, as Tim recalled it, until he was nineteen, after he'd started college. Little things, like some of his classmates, some in a huff, asking him why he hadn't spoken to them when they passed on the campus. Tim had no memory of being in the places where they said they saw him. It happened too often for him to disregard it. He finally made an appointment with a professor of psychology and had a long talk with the man. The professor put him to every test he could devise, and his opinion of the phenomena was that it was a case of bilocation. You are where you are, but you are seen someplace else. Maybe you will shortly show up in the place where you were seen, where you weren't, but you weren't there when you were seen!

Tim was pawed over by most of the scientific community for quite awhile, until he finally stopped talking about it, just wanting to be left alone. After graduating from college, Tim got a job with an insurance company in San Francisco. He did well in his work, and within a year and a half, met and married Carolyn. His bilocative excursions had been quiescent, at least he'd not been approached for awhile and accused of being seen somewhere he hadn't been, so he didn't mention any of this to Carolyn.

Things were pretty status quo for about two more years, then one day Carolyn called him at the office and wanted to know if something was wrong? She'd seen him in the garage, and wanted to know why he didn't come into the house? And how had he gotten back to the office so soon, she'd just seen him ten minutes ago? The office was almost a half-hour trip from the house. Tim hadn't been out of the office for three hours. The time had come; he had to face it. He went right home, damning whatever it was within, or without, him. As carefully and honestly as possible, he explained the whole thing to Carolyn. Thank goodness, some people can accept the unexplained and not go into a state of shocked disbelief or fall over backwards.

I might add that Carolyn is a Gemini, and I have found that sign to be the most open, or interested in the new, the bizarre; Gemini like strange things; it titillates their unusually quick minds; they go along with it. She went along with it—got books and read what was known of this particular phenomenon.

Occasionally, one of their friends would remark about having seen Tim somewhere, and that when they went over to speak to him, he either turned around and got lost in a crowd or just disappeared. The friends who didn't and couldn't believe soon dropped away. To them Tim was a spook, and they would have none of it.

Carolyn treated it as some kind of delightful joke on Tim, that is, until one day when Tim came home, white-faced, and announced that he'd seen Mr. H—, who had died about a month previous. Not only had he seen him, but Mr. H—, had talked to him, *and he had talked to Mr. H—!* To add to the confusion, when Tim *met* Mr. H—, he, Tim, had been in his own office, but the meeting took place in a downtown building where the deceased Mr. H— had worked when alive. It would seem to be enough to have bilocation, but when the bilocation extends to conversing with "dead" people, the interest is compounded and it "gets pretty hairy," which is the way Tim put it.

How would you like to live in constant expectation of someone approaching you and accusing you of being someplace you have no knowledge of being? How would you feel if you found yourself talking with someone who'd been pronounced dead, and who'd been buried, and there they were just as "real" as when they'd been ambling around in a physical body? It bothered Tim considerably more because this was the first instance in which he *remembered* having had a conversation in a place where he hadn't been, let alone where the conversant was physically dead.

It's uncomfortable enough just to have the phenomena, but when one works for a highly circumspect institution like an insurance company, that wishes to garner the respect and confidence of the public, it does get pretty hairy if one of their employees gets to be known as a kook.

It is known the possibility exists that different fractions of the personality can act so far independently of each other that one is not conscious of the other's actions. That doesn't mean the individual isn't "normal" in most all respects. A conscious bilocation is as simple as sitting in a classroom, and being out fishing at the same time or up in the mountains skiing. The instructor's voice brings you back, but you were *there*. The scene is as vivid as though it is actually happening. It doesn't do much for your grades at exam time, but you've actually been in two places at once. Some call it day-dreaming.

Tim doesn't know what to do about his "gift." Hypnotism hasn't seemed to help. The Dicksons have a little girl now, and one thing neither of them wants is for her to grow up with other children telling her that their dad says her dad is a nut.

No Sir Arthur Conan Doyles, no Houdinis come through, appear to him. The ghosts he meets in his bilocations are usually former "solid" members of the community. He's not solved any crimes, exposed any murderers, found any buried treasure by receiving word from someone on the other side who professes to know about such things. He's made copious notes on the travels and conversations with discarnates, and sometime, after he retires, he says he wants to write a book, put the whole thing down for public consumption. Perhaps by that time there will be more acceptance, or at least partial acceptance by those who scientifically, mentally, and emotionally face the facts about survival and our close connection with those who've "passed over."

My own reaction has been a tendency to take a second look at a lot of people when I meet or pass them! I never know when I might see someone who is there, but isn't there. Who knows? Things really aren't what they seem; anyhow, so I'm told by those who are supposed to know.

Hello, Deer

We've not had anything on excarnate animals appearing here and there, and it's true that they, like humans, show up at their familiar haunts after physical death.

The materialization of excarnate human beings is well established. There is abundant evidence of the replay of the human memory tape of time, showing scenes of old buildings, wagon trains, tree-lined streets, troopers and Indians fighting it out, long-dead people walking about. Animals, too, have their memory of life, existing in their astral or cosmic body. I've listened to many stories of animal materializations, but only two are empirical, that is, have been testified to by more than one person.

One concerns a cocker spaniel who would materialize and run about the house, sniffing out familiar people, places, and things. It was seen by two members of the same family, not by the other three, and a hot controversy waged regarding who was putting who on! If it had only lifted its excarnate leg against a chair and left some physical evidence, the story would bear more credence!

Man's search for continuing life is concerned mostly with himself and other humans. Therefore I find it efficacious to include in the record what I know of one animal, the deer of Sheep Springs.

The postmaster of Cantil, California, one Martin Engel, has resided in the area for some forty-five years. Martin began his desert sojourn as a prospector right out of school, then studied for and became an assayer. The vanishing breed of old-time assayers have been referred to as a midwife to the prospector and his hoped-for birth of a fortune. Martin is the font of knowledge for this section of the desert when it comes to local news.

Nearby is an area called Kelso Valley. It, like most of the region, is bleak, windy, and remote—murderously hot in the summer, very cold in the winter. It is spotted here and there with the copses of canebrake, tumbleweed, and creosote bushes surrounding waterholes. When water is found, chances are a human has taken advantage of it, moved in, erected some sort of dwelling and tried to do some farming.

Such a spot was found by an Indian named Henry. He's about forty, has lived in Kelso Valley for a good part of his adult life, wrenching a hard living from the adobe-like earth. Henry, like most of the Indians (and I can't blame them) is pretty close-mouthed about his superstitions, the placement of mineral deposits, or even about divulging Indian lore of the area. The fabled incidents of Indians being beaten, tortured, and killed by whites in the "old days," often over the whereabouts of gold and silver, would, could, and at times still are being repeated today. Over a period of two years, Henry has accepted Martin to the extent of dropping little tidbits of information.

The Deer of Sheep Springs isn't unknown to the inhabitants of the Mojave, but Henry was, and is, a first-hand spectator. This deer is huge, much larger than any other deer ever seen by the hunters. It's been fired on from a distance and from close up, with and without a scope-mounted rifle. When deer season opens up, the whole desert becomes a happy hunting ground . . . for the hunters, that is. The deer usually take to the mountains and crags to escape annihilation by doughty "sportsmen." Henry has also fired at the deer from close up, many times. He knows for sure his bullets have found the mark, but each time the animal has disappeared into the canebrake surrounding the Sheep Springs; and diligent search has never turned up so much as a blood smear, broken branch, or hoofprint, any one of which a wounded animal that size would surely leave. The antler spread would alone prevent the deer from entering the copse.

This phenomenon has been observed by dozens of hunters over the past thirty-five years. Groups have actually set out with one thought in mind, to surround the Springs, find the Deer, and shoot or capture it, but this has never been accomplished. The deer, when disturbed, or shot at, takes off into the Sheep Springs cane and is not seen again. Henry has accompanied such groups, and stands by as they go through the same rigamarole he's been through year after year: shoot; the Deer runs into the copse; the hunters surround it; enter; beat the brush; look for a carcass, caves, or niches; and come out completely baffled, sadder, wiser, dumbfounded, and empty-handed. It's enough to make a man take to strong drink!

Henry told Martin that when he sees the Deer nowadays, he doesn't shoot at it or chase it, he just smiles at it and says "Hello, Deer," and stands by to watch hunters shoot and chase "the Deer that isn't there." If this deer has lived to the extreme age of thirty-five, or more, as it would seem, it could hardly be expected to even tote the fantastic set of antlers it allegedly carries, let alone run into the canebrake without becoming hopelessly entangled in the dense growth, and would be easily captured or killed. Expert trackers from hundreds of miles away have made the trek to Sheep Springs to either dispel the myth, or bring out the animal. It hasn't been done, yet. How can you capture a ghost?

Hey, Mule!

John Sturgeon takes us off on a story of an animal who was still present, following its physical death.

"Well, there was one time I remember real well. I was about seventeen, and worked at the old Standard Mine, up there in Bodie. That was about 1901 or 1902. The mine manager was a Cornishman named Johnny Bolton. He always gave the young guys a chance to work, the local boys.

"There were several men killed in the mine, like Hicks and Curnan and Thompson. After they died, I never heard any stories of them haunting the mine, but there was a big white mule they worked on the 500-foot level in the mine. One day a line of mine cars broke loose and ran down the track, ran right into the mule and broke its back, and they had to kill it. They hauled it back near the main shaft and buried it in a deep hole they had dug all the ore out of, put all the loose rock, sand and gravel in on top of it.

"One day, about a couple of weeks later, I guess, one of my friends, Johnny Cruz, was pushing one of the smaller hand ore cars up the track on the 500-foot level, cleaning up any rock that had fallen off the bigger cars as they took the ore out. All of a sudden, when he was pushing the car, it stopped, and he couldn't push it anymore. He went around in front and looked under the wheels and couldn't find anything blocking them. He went back and tried to push the car again, and it seemed to him there was something pushing against it from the other end. When he let go of the car, it would roll back about three feet and then stop. He would push it up again, it would be stopped, then he would let it go and it would only roll back about three feet. The track was level there and there wasn't any reason for the car to roll either way. He walked around the car and headed toward the main shaft, to go up and get somebody to help him.

"When that mule had been worked, it had a whiffle tree hooked up to its harness, and one of the things we used it for was to haul timbers along the track by a timber chain attached to the whiffle tree. As Johnny walked up the track, right there in front of him was this timber chain. It was moving along between the tracks, like a snake, but there wasn't anything attached to either end of it! That scared Johnny a lot, and he ran back down the stope a ways and just stood there, wondering what to do.

"There wasn't a sound in the tunnel but that chain rattling along the ground on the ties and stones between the tracks. The noise stopped, and Johnny went back for another look. The chain was gone. Well, he came up topside and told me what happened. I went back down with him, and we looked all over the place. We found the chain about one hundred feet from the ore car Johnny had been working with. It was lying right where the mule stayed when we weren't working it, just lying there on the ground.

"That scared Johnny so bad he quit a few days later. He was convinced that mule was still there. Other miners who hadn't heard about it, came up after that and told they had seen the chain snaking along between the tracks. Two of those fellows quit; they refused to go on that 500-foot level.

"I never saw the chain move, but when I was down there one day, all alone, I felt like there was something near me, then I smelled fresh mule droppings. I looked all over but couldn't find any. And that mule had been dead for maybe six months by that time. Old droppings don't smell like fresh ones. I didn't even stay around any longer.

"Years later I heard that some other miners in the old Standard reported they had actually seen a white mule on the 500-foot level. I guess he just got used to it there and doesn't want to leave."

On a recent trip to Bridgeport, I learned that John Sturgeon passed into spirit March 12, 1970, at the age of eighty-five.

Talkative Ghosts

I'm Still
with You

The attractive blonde woman absolutely refused to turn and look at the apparition of her long-dead mother when she was told by her friend it was standing off to the left and just behind her, smiling at her. It's never happened to me, so I don't know whether I would have looked either! I can't blame her for not looking, except she missed a great opportunity.

Why is it that some people have more psychic ability to see spirits than others? Astrological charts have been drawn up on most of the known mediums and psychics, here and abroad, and they all come up with a similar set of indications. If an individual has certain planets located particularly in the twelfth house of their zodiacal chart, chances are that they will be interested in and have psychic ability. Those with what is called "loaded" twelfth house are definitely psychic, and possibly mediumistic.

One of the ladies we deal with in this story, my wife, Florence, has just such a chart. Her twelfth house isn't loaded, but contains the psychic planets. She doesn't have the ability all the time, but when, due to the progressions, squares, conjunctions, trines, or the ticking off of those psychic planets, she enters into a period when psychic phenomena become clear and real to her, she is then receptive—a receiver, a perceiver. When the transit is over, she doesn't have the ability, no matter how hard she might try to push it.

Florence is a Gemini: slender, dark-haired, quick, and manually expressive—the opposite of her friend, Helen. Helen is a Capricorn: serious of nature, blonde, medium height, sometimes giving the impression of being indifferent, withdrawn.

The girls had been friends for perhaps a year. Both had lived in the San Fernando Valley (an area near Los Angeles) for over five years, knew something about one another. Helen moved to the Valley some years after her mother passed away. Florence states that she had never met the mother, had never seen a photo of her, in fact had only heard her mentioned very infrequently.

One evening the two girls took a night off, had dinner together at a restaurant. Afterwards they returned to Helen's apartment, where they just sat around talking. Helen had been depressed for some time, and Florence, hoping to cheer her up, was chatting about local gossip, Helen's boy friends, the weather—you name it. Finally, Helen began to tell Florence her deeper feelings, how hopelessly she viewed her life. This got them into a discussion of the relative merits of life versus death, staying here or stopping the planet so one could get off.

I must interject here that Helen's mother, now an excarnate spirit, was a psychic medium during her lifetime, allowing herself to be psychically "used" by others, at no charge (although she was very poor), whenever they asked her to do so. Helen loved her mother deeply, but when, as a little girl, she witnessed her mother's trances and heard the alleged mediumistic utterances, she was ashamed, and her reaction was one of total rejection of the entire concept of mediumship. However, she had not forgotten certain mani-festations that had occurred, utterances which had been made during her mother's delivery of otherworld messages.

The evening was cool, but not cold. The doors and windows were shut. Florence began to complain of a terrible chill in the room, and got up to put on a sweater she'd brought with her. Then she began to rub her arms briskly, then her legs, and finally got up again to locate the draft. She explained that it was like standing in front of the blast from a refrigerated air conditioner. Helen watched her friend's behavior in silence, then asked, "I wonder if my mother knew she was going to die the night that she did?"

Florence was seated now, facing Helen as the following happened. Florence answered at once, "Yes, Anna——, knew; that is why she said the things to you that she did before she went to her bedroom."

Florence had just given not only information completely unknown to her, but she'd given the maiden name of Helen's mother, who'd been married four times! Helen told me later that she was certain Florence knew nothing of seances. Recognizing the familiar "chill" manifestation she'd witnessed during her mother's trances, Helen then asked many questions, and Florence, still rubbing her freezing skin, with teeth almost chattering, gave answers that meant nothing to her, but had great meaning to Helen. Finally, Florence said, "There's your mother, right over there. Turn around and say hello, she's grinning!"

Helen didn't turn around, but instead, staring steadily at Florence, asked, "What does she look like?"

The answer came immediately. "She has a figure like an hour glass, about five feet tall, although she has no feet; I can't see her feet; her hair is light brown and frizzly-curly all over, like a child's. She's wearing horn-rimmed glasses. Her dress is white and there's a very wide brown leather belt around her waist."

Helen still didn't turn, but said, "Yes, that is my mother," and continued to ask questions. Quite impatiently now, Florence told Helen to ask her own questions. "She's smiling at you, turn around, ask her yourself."

Finally the vision faded. It had been present about forty minutes. All during this time Florence had been literally freezing, but only, as she put it, on the skin surface, with a kind of "upheaving" feeling around her torso, especially along her back. During the time of the appearance of the apparition, she did not find any of the situation unusual or strange, except for the chilling. Seeing the woman standing there seemed quite normal.

After the vision faded, so did Florence's chills. It was only then that Helen told Florence that this was to have been their last visit together. She had planned to take her own life that night, and had indeed bought some potent sleeping pills when she'd visited downtown Los Angeles. Now that her mother had appeared, it left no doubt in her mind that the mother knew of her intent, and had "come back" to reassure her, give her renewed hope that committing suicide was not the way to solve what appeared to be insufferable personal problems.

Helen said that it was Florence's initial mention of her mother's maiden name that convinced her she had been wrong about the mother's mediumistic abilities and the possibility of life after death. The two friends met for the next few nights in an attempt to recreate the event, and although Florence would suffer the terrible chills and give answers to

Helen's questions, the materialization of the mother never happened again.

Finally, Florence could take the chills no longer and told Helen to go "direct," which Helen subsequently did try to do, but whether because the need was never again so great, or because Helen's psychic ability wasn't enough, which is probably the answer, she was not successful.

Here we have the instance of an excarnate relative, a mother in this case, showing intimate knowledge of her daughter's thoughts and actions, and in this time of trial, or peril, appearing through the mediumistic ability of another to bring support and comfort—communicating to the effect that life doesn't end with the physical death.

Florence's own mother passed on about eight months later, and in prayer and meditation, Florence would ask for some word from her. Two months after her mother's death, a friend from Los Angeles called her and told her she had visited a psychic woman in the San Fernando Valley, and right in the middle of the reading for herself, the woman stopped and said she "had a message for a friend named Florence: Florence's mother would appear at Florence's bedside—Florence would know what she meant. The time was not now." The psychic didn't know Florence, had never heard of her, and the friend was not consciously thinking of Florence at the time of the sitting.

I'm very grateful to Helen for telling me the story, talking to me about it. There is a certain onus connected to people who talk about seeing or communicating with spirits! I talk openly to anyone about phenomena; but then I'm an actor, and everyone knows those "show people" are kookie.

Recently there have been articles in the press about how so many "show people" run their lives by astrology, the inordinate interest they show in the subject. That's true, and it's also true that astrology has become a multibillion dollar industry for the manufacture of almost everything which can be lumped under the purview of the zodiac!

Yes, I'm kookie enough to be investigatively interested in astrology, psychic phenomena, telepathy, continuing life, spiritualism, card reading, palmistry, crystal ball gazing, head reading, and foot reading (did you know about that one?), tea leaf reading, numerology, Ouija boards, flying saucers, clairaudience, clairvoyance, levitation, mutation, automatic writing, automatic speech, ecstasy, hypnotism, astral projection, witches, magic, hallucination, phantasms of the living and the dead, motor automatisms, trance and possession, multiplex personalities (so dear to the heart of psychologists), any sensory automatisms, ectoplasm, and genius. Many of the above could have been lumped under the heading of ESP, or Metapsychics, but writing it out gives the neophyte an idea of the scope of what we are talking about.

I am not consciously psychic, although it is well established that most of us do have some psychic ability, whether we like it or not! We just don't recognize it for what it is. My best method, at this point, of getting in touch or in tune with any of the above is to sit with those who do have the ability; and I do it all, as I've said, in an investigative manner, wanting to be shown and hoping to keep an open mind in the process. And, let me add right here, I believe in a little prayer to ward off any evil!

A warning about playing around with astrology with other people. If someone completely negates anything smacking of

astrology, (continuing life, ghosts, etc.), becomes apoplecti-
cally furious when the subject is brought up, his own astrological chart would no doubt show that it could be mentally
and emotionally dangerous, if not fatal, for that individual to
believe in anything he can't see, touch, or taste.

My Own
Personal Ghost

Did you ever visit a psychic? In 1966 I visited a woman clairvoyant. It was my first experience, and I certainly didn't know what to expect.

Not so many years ago, she would have been called a witch, a succubus, a crone, a hag, pictured popularly as being clad in long, flowing skirts which hid voluminous pockets containing herbs, bones, potions, philters, bent almost double, possessed of a long angular nose with huge warts on it. Had she been caught in those fine olden days, she would have been brought before the assize, subjected to unspeakable tortures, maligned, pilloried, and, like as not, hanged or burned publicly. Today such people are called psychics, or sensitives; they have been endowed with a physical body referred to as a "loose vehicle of vitality," so made up that it can be used by excarnate spirits to make vocal contact and bring messages from the other side. They are in cosmic tune.

In a large segment of our population, even today, the image of a psychic, a person dealing in the occult, is related to the centuries of persecution of those benighted souls, achieving its ghastly pinnacle in the 1600s. Some of those brought to trial, horribly tortured, and put to death, were undoubtedly psychic, some insane, some self-deluded, others trying to save themselves by confessing to the heinous crimes with which they were charged. Because of their alleged acts, the charge of witchcraft, and the manner in which they were charged with doing it, the Church was a front-runner, charging them with the crime of heresy, going to the depths of lies, intolerance, and extreme cruelty. Hitler's persecution of the Jews in the twentieth century is much the same. Undoubtedly, some few were psychic, possessed powers of divination. The famous Witch of Endor, for example, was a psychic. When King Saul, during a seance with the witch, was told that Samuel was present in spirit, he asked for a description, and upon receiving it and recognizing it as Samuel, threw himself down upon the ground in an attitude of supplication. Samuel told Saul that he would be defeated by the Philistines, and that he would die. The Witch of Endor performed what is called necromancy, a method of divination, a crime punishable by torture and death. Saul had promised beforehand he wouldn't rat on her, and he kept his word!

On February 8, 1966, I showed up for my first sitting with Mrs. Cawforth (not her real name, as she wishes to remain anonymous at the level of the press). The woman who answered the door and invited me in was most pleasant, attractive, dark-haired, in her middle thirties. She ushered me into the kitchen and indicated for me to be seated at a small round table. I took a cup of coffee, she seated herself opposite me, and we just talked for a moment. Then she reached under the table and whipped out an Ouija board and placed it on the table between us. She placed her hand on the three-pronged planchette and began moving it rapidly back and forth, up and down the board.

"Have you ever had a sitting before?"

"Yes, frequently."

"Well, let's see if you have someone working with you on the other side who can come through today."

I sat with folded arms, not touching the table nor the board. Then she began to speak, rapidly. "Yes, yes. I am Louis. I worked with you at the studio. You were very friendly. I fell. I hit my head."

Her hand stopped and she asked me if I knew the one coming through, Louis? I was so nonplussed at the rapidity with which the whole thing was happening I couldn't recall having known anyone by that name. We sat for awhile as I tried to recollect. Then I locked in. I had known a fellow called Louis about fourteen years ago. It was when I was playing the role of Captain Midnight in a TV series filmed by Screen Gems, in Hollywood, for CBS-TV airing to the six million fans and members of the Secret Squadron. The man who was the stunt double for my sidekick, Ichabod Mudd (with two d's!), was named Louie, and I told this to the psychic. Her hand moved quickly over the board almost before I'd gotten the words out of my mouth. "Yes, yes. I am Louie. I am glad you have come to communicate."

She paused again and asked me about the story of Louie. Previously, he'd been a race driver, I understand, at Indianapolis. He had an accident which prevented him from ever race driving again, had come to Hollywood, and had gotten into stunt work for the studios. Louie had been a very pleasant, vital little fellow, quick, athletic, a good conversationalist, always ready for a joke or some horseplay. I liked him a lot. We had fun and games around the set between takes, and had lunch together frequently. The "Midnight" series took a two-week hiatus, and Louie filled in by getting a job at another studio. He and some other stunt man set up a fight scene in the wheel house of a ship, rehearsed it, then filmed it. Louie misjudged during the fight action, went over backwards, hit his head on a sharp projection, and was in a coma for a week. During that week, I called the hospital and was told that he could not receive calls or visitors. The next word I received was that he had not survived the operation to relieve the pressure on his brain caused by the fall. I was quite shook up over his death. Over the years I would from time to time fondly remember Louie, but the memory of him had waned and I'd not consciously thought of him for at least three or four years. "I am Louis, I worked with you at the studio. You were very friendly. I fell. I hit my head!"

The man who had given me Mrs. Cawforth's phone number hadn't known about Louie. Mrs. Cawforth had no connection with the studios. She'd worked in a laundry in some town in Arizona, had married a man from Southern California, and now lived in the San Fernando Valley. Now she was asking me if I had any questions to ask Louie? I'd not come prepared for anything like this, someone I had known coming through with the evidence Louie had just laid on me. What do you ask?

"Where are you, Louie?"

"He's right here," said Mrs. Cawforth, moving the planchette over the board.

"Where?"

"In the room, near you."

(Crazy, man.)

"Your questions, please," she repeated.

"What are you doing, Louie?" I asked, rather brilliantly, I hoped.

Mrs. Cawforth's hand moved quickly with the planchette.

She spoke in her own voice. "I am glad you have come to communicate. I am working with you on your back problem. I am protecting you in the desert, in the mountains."

She stopped for a moment. "Do you have a back problem?"

I answered in the affirmative. In 1962 I was almost totally incapacitated for the entire year with arthritis of the spine. Since then, with various medications and exercise, I've been able to function quite normally, but must at all times guard against quick turns or bending. For all intents and purposes, unless one knew my personal history, the problem was not apparent either in walking, running, or climbing mountains. Then she asked if I went to the desert, the mountains?

"Yes." For twenty-five years I've been a desert and mountain explorer. Most often I go it alone, with my dog for company, in a jeep or four-wheel drive station wagon. I climb mountains, slide down precipitous hills, crawl into old mine shafts.

"Have you ever been hurt while you were out there?"

"No, never."

"Question?"

"Thanks, Louie, for your help. How are things in the mountains?"

"I like the place where you are working. There is some lead there, some silver, not much of value, but it makes you happy. It is good for you to go. It is cold at night where you stay, there is no heat. I am not cold here."

I do have a claim in Panamint Valley, California, about two hundred miles from Los Angeles, and go up there frequently. Assay reports show there is "some lead there, some silver, not much of value. . . ."

"Is there anything of value there?"

"No, not there."

"Where?"

"Up the canyon from where you are."

Then he began what I later *came to understand* was his "sign-off." "The communication is growing dim. The woman is getting tired. I like the leather nook in your kitchen. I am with you. You are blessed. God bless you."

I do have a leather nook in my kitchen! Mrs. Cawforth has never been in my house.

My wife was doing some housework when I got home. I called her into the kitchen and related the whole story of the sitting, all about Louie. She had never met Louie. Her eyes were wide with wonder but not disbelief.

A few days later I was sitting in my kitchen talking with actor Clint Walker ("Cheyenne," *The Great Bank Robbery*), telling him about the sitting. He just sat, chin in hand, and watched me. We'd never discussed anything like this before, and I felt I wasn't getting through to him. When I'd finished, he sat for a moment, then said, "Yeah. When can I have a sitting with the woman?" He explained that it wasn't because he either believed or disbelieved; he wanted to find out for himself, like most of us.

I got busy doing some television shows, appearing in three feature movies, and it was a year before I called Mrs. Cawforth for another sitting. She was booked solid, so I made an appointment for the following week. In the week before the sitting, my wife and I drove to Fresno, California, to visit some friends. We took Interstate 14 and 58 through Mojave to Bakersfield, California. On arriving in Bakersfield, the weather was nasty, raining, misty. Three roads merge from different directions and finally hookup with the north-south freeway system through Bakersfield. Leaving my wife in the car, I went into a little restaurant to get some coffee for us. Casually, as one does, I noted that the waitress was rather short, dark-haired, heavyset. After she'd given me the coffee, I asked directions to the freeway to Fresno.

"Everybody gets lost here. Come here, I'll show you." She walked with me to the front of the restaurant and pointed out how I could get onto the right street to the freeway, and I left.

The next week I had the sitting with Mrs. Cawforth. By this time, I'd made a list of questions I wanted to ask Louie, if he came through. It had been a long time. The sitting began as the first one had; her hand moved quickly over the Ouija board.

"Yes. I am here. This is Louis. I am glad you have come to communicate. I have been with you."

I then asked some of the questions I'd brought along, to which I received answers which couldn't be checked out. Then I asked what turned out to be the sixty-four-dollar question.

"Are there people on this planet from another planet?"

"Yes."

"Have I ever met one?"

"Yes."

"Where? When?"

"On your trip north, you stopped at a coffee shop to ask directions. The woman behind the counter was short, dark, heavyset. Her name is Florence." I'd not made any mention of any trip, anywhere, to Mrs. Cawforth, let alone that I'd stopped in a coffee shop to ask directions! Suddenly Mrs. Cawforth broke in.

"There is something else coming here. Yes. Yes. Nizam, a holy man of India has just died. He cannot contact you yet, but he will soon. You knew one another in a former life. He will help you when he awakens."

"When will I hear of his death?"

"You will read about it in the newspaper. Within three days. It is a small article. You must look." Then the "sign-off" came and the session ended with Louie's telling me he was with me, to come again. I found that Mrs. Cawforth could sustain her powers for about thirty to thirty-five minutes, then she seemed to grow tired, lose vitality. What amazed me was the fact that I'd not had a sitting for a year, and my friend Louie immediately came through. Mrs. Cawforth has sometimes three or four sittings a day. How in the world could she so accurately remember the names of excarnates for each individual, unless she has the most amazing memory in history.

Here were two choice tidbits to check out. (1) Was the woman in the restaurant named Florence? (2) Could I find an article in the paper about some Nizam? That sitting was at 4:30 P.M., March 22, 1967. The next morning I carefully went over every page in the *Los Angeles Times,* looking for some possible squib or article about a Nizam. The following day was the same, no printed word about Nizam dying. The third day, Saturday, March 25, 1967, on page 8 of the *LA Times* I found this article: "Nizam of Hyderabad Dies in Indian Palace: One of the Richest Men in World, He Claimed Descent From Prophet Mohammed." It went on to relate the circumstances of his death, the size of his domain, and the name of his successor. At once I called Burbank airport and inquired about the time differential between here and Hyderabad, India. It is approximately thirteen hours. Figuring back, the only mathematical conclusion my wife and I could arrive at was that Nizam had died between 4:30 P.M. and 5 P.M., during the day I was having the sitting with Mrs. Cawforth! Unless she had a powerful shortwave radio that would pick up worldwide news immediately, there was no possible way for her to have known of the death. I also called a friend of mine at the CBS News Room in Hollywood, and asked him, without divulging why, if he would check and see if any word of the death of the Nizam of Hyderabad had been received from their news contacts in India during the day of the twenty-second. He checked all the files and records, called me back to report no findings, and asked why I wanted to know. Not being sure of what his feelings or reactions might be to things supernatural or occult, I didn't go into the Ouija board and psychics, merely told him a friend had thought he picked it up on his shortwave radio, then read of it, wanted to find out. Lame, but it seemed sufficient. He said that if the article was on page 8, it indicated the reporters over there didn't think it of too great news value, and it probably wouldn't have been immediately beamed out.

Subsequently, when I visited Mrs. Cawforth again, I came right out and asked her what radio equipment she had in the house, and she let me look into the two bedrooms and the front room. The common, small house radio and one small TV set were all she had.

Now there remained the question of "Florence," the woman from another planet, in the restaurant in Bakersfield. My wife's name is Florence, and I wondered if Mrs. Cawforth had picked this up from my mind. It was a couple of months before I could find time to get to Bakersfield. Then, in company with a geologist friend, we drove to Bakersfield, taking the same route in as my wife and I had on the trip to Fresno.

The restaurant was still there. We went in, seated ourselves. I didn't see the waitress who'd served me on the first visit, and when our waitress came to take our orders, I asked her if Florence was working that day?

"Florence? She quit last month."

"Wasn't she kinda short and heavyset?"

"Yeah. I thought you knew her?"

"I only know her name. She waited on me once before. Do you know where she went?"

"No. Waitresses come and go here."

"Do you know where she lived?"

"She rented a room, somewhere. I don't know."

That was all. But her name was Florence!

From the story thus far, you can imagine I was feeling a bit frustrated. A woman from another planet! Let's take a look at the evidentials so far.

1. Yes, I had worked with a Louie at the studio. We had been very friendly. He'd fallen, hit his head, had died as the result of it.
2. I am working a small claim that yields lead and silver, not much of value.
3. I do have a leather nook in my kitchen.
4. I did find the article in the newspaper about the Nizam, within three days, as I was told.
5. I had met a dark, heavyset woman on my trip north, in a restaurant, and she'd given me directions. She was supposed to be from another planet, her name was Florence.

Two weeks later I talked Mrs. Cawforth into another sitting. One of the questions I asked Louie was, "Who had originally owned a mine high up the mountain near where my claim is?"

I'd checked the claim but found no markers or monuments containing names of anyone who might have worked it. Without hesitation, through Mrs. Cawforth, the answer came, "Adams and Becker."

I asked the year? No answer. I asked what they were looking for? No answer. Now I was saddled with Adams and Becker! It had to be checked out.

My wife and I knew a couple, Les and Ruth Cooper, who lived at a place called Dunmovin, California. It's on State Route 395, thirty miles south of Lone Pine, California, in the Sierra Nevadas. They are both attorneys and conduct their practice from Dunmovin. Les has specialized in mining law, and has extensive mining claims of his own. Both of them are interested in metaphysics. If anyone could appreciate what I was involved with they could. We drove to Dunmovin, told them what I had received from Louie, and said we wanted to go to Independence, California, the county seat, to try and find Adams and Becker in the mining books, principally to check out Mrs. Cawforth, through whom all this was allegedly coming. They immediately agreed, and off we went.

Those mining claim books are huge things, five inches thick. Ruth and my wife took a book each, as did Les and I. Two hours later both women had given up, and were just sitting, talking. Les and I were both looking in the same book, one of the older ones. Finally, as I turned the page, at the top, on the first line, was "Adams, C.L.!" the name of the mine, its location (which I'd written down from a mining map of the area), and the coordinates. The year was 1901! Les looked at me, eyes wide. "Are you surprised? That's it!"

"Not surprised, really. Where is Becker?"

Now I had number six spike in the rail of verified information received from Louie, from the other side, through

Mrs. Cawforth. There had been a mass of misinformation, too. Many of the things told me have in no way come true. With the investigations I've done the past couple of years, it appears that even the best psychic, or medium, can receive wrong information; or some of them out and out get involved in falsehoods under the guise of having received information from some occult source; or, in order to fill in the time of the sitting, tell a sitter what they think he wants to hear. But, it only takes *one* white crow to prove all crows aren't black! And I feel there have been enough white crows through Mrs. Cawforth, from Louie, to prove the validity of this form of communication.

In April, 1968, actor John Agar and I made a motion picture in Dallas, Texas. While there, I visited a Negro psychic, Mrs. Murdock, who uses a deck of playing cards to concentrate with and "listen." Just a few moments after she began our sitting, she looked up at me with a little smile. "You've got somebody working with you on the other side, they go around with you, don't they?"

"Yes, they do." I was careful not to supply any verbal information, and tried to keep my mind a blank. What she could pick up from my subconscious or unconscious was something else. She continued to throw down the cards with her long, slim, well manicured hands. "His name is—(more cards)—Louie, isn't it?" Her eyes seemed to bore into me, her forehead was wrinkled with a slight frown.

"That's right."

"Anything you want to ask him?"

"Yes. Hello, Louie. How are we doing?"

She sat for a moment, slowly throwing down the cards three at a time. "He says he's glad you came to talk with him. The communication is coming better."

She went silent for a time, then continued, "You are going out of the country to make a film. It is Mexico. It is the first time. You will go, the picture will not be made."

Other things told me were not evidential, were trivial in nature, and the sitting was over. There had been no indication or offer of a film out of the country, either to me or through my agent. Shortly after returning to Los Angeles, a month later to be exact, in checking my diary, I was signed to make a movie in Mexico City. It was the first time I'd had an offer to make a picture out of the country. I did go to Mexico, the picture was not made due to money difficulties, and we returned to Los Angeles. Spike number seven in favor of Louie!

On June 4, 1968, my wife, Florence, had a sitting with Mrs. Cawforth. During the session, Louie broke in to tell her that I would undergo head surgery before the end of the month that would be beneficial. At 11:30 P.M., June 23, 1968, I was playing penny ante poker with some friends in Northridge, California, when I suddenly began to feel very groggy, my gums started swelling. At 2 A.M. of the twenty-fourth, I was sitting in a dentist's office undergoing deep emergency surgery in the "head" for a dangerous gum condition I'd not been aware of. It was beneficial. The eighth verifiable from Louie.

In August, 1968, I stopped off in New Orleans, on my way to Miami, to visit some long-time friends. Whenever I'm going to be in an area for a few days, I try to find out if there is a psychic around, and if possible have a sitting with them. Of the sixteen psychics, sensitives, card readers, tea leaf readers, and palm readers I've visited in the past few years, I would say five of them have given me information which could possibly be checked out to my satisfaction.

A waiter at The Court of Two Sisters, in the French Quarter, whispered a name and address to me when I queried him about a psychic. Fortune-telling, as it is called, is illegal in Louisiana, as it is in most states, and actually with good reason. There are too many charlatans. The woman I met with at the address on Beacon Street, New Orleans, was a crystal ball gazer, but her crystal ball had been stolen and she was using a glass tumbler full of water! She sat looking into the glass for a few moments.

"You have come from some distance." (That's a safe bet.)

"Yes."

"There is someone who is near you, a man in spirit." (This could be safely said to anyone.)

"That's true. Do you know who it is?" I asked.

"He stays very close to you but cannot communicate directly." (Also safe.)

"That's true."

"His name is Lawrence, no . . . Larry . . . Louie." Target!

"Hello, Louie."

"You know him?"

"Yes. What does he say?"

"He is glad you came to talk. He says you will return to the mountains very soon to do some writing. He will be with you. It is a good idea." Then she launched into some mundane stuff which I recognized to be filler. I thanked her when the reading was over, donated three dollars toward a new crystal ball, and left.

I had not started the writing at that time, but was thinking a lot about it and wanted to get into the Sierra Nevadas to get some stories about ghosts up there. I was glad to hear Louie thought it was a good idea! The ninth thing Louie seemed to know about. The water glass gazer was the third psychic Louie had come through. Would I continue to disbelieve?

That completes *My Own Personal Ghost,* which is, to this point, material I've received from Louie through psychics, mostly Mrs. Cawforth. One last anecdote regarding Mrs. Cawforth's clairvoyance. An actor friend, a leading male star, was told through her that he would be shot at over land during a personal appearance trip to an aircraft carrier stationed off Vietnam. He made the trip to the carrier, and was then flown to the battle area. The helicopter was fired at "over land," and they got out of there.

Arthur Ford, the world-renowned trance-medium, has a "control" spirit named Fletcher who has worked with Arthur for about fifty years. Arthur has been subjected to exhaustive tests by all the leading psychic researchers in this and other countries, and has been stamped authentic in every case; he has had sittings with top federal officials and with a great many of the crowned heads of Europe. Reverend Ford had some televised sittings with the late Bishop James Pike, during which time trance—medium contact was made with the Bishop's late son and information divulged to the Bishop which Reverend Ford would have no way of knowing. Bishop Pike, in his book, *The Other Side,* has written extensively on those and sittings with other mediums.

When I visited Mr. Ford in New Haven, Connecticut, earlier in the year, he was working on his latest book, *Unknown But Known.* He said he was going to California on a lecture tour for Spiritual Frontiers Fellowship, and I invited him to the house for dinner. He accepted, and upon his arrival in Los Angeles, on November 14, I picked him up at the Ambassador Hotel, and brought him out to my house.

Also present at the dinner, in addition to my wife and I, were actor Clint Walker and his girl friend and a geologist friend of ours. To my everlasting sorrow, Arthur was not able to do any trance work at the time. A muscular constriction around his heart, which has subsequently been corrected, prevented him from going "out of body," as he does in trance, to enable Fletcher to take over his vocal mechanism and bring messages from the other side. We did get him to reminisce about his life as a medium, about seances, spirit visitations, materializations, manifestations, ectoplasmic exudations, as well as astral projections. I don't know and can't speak for the others who were present, but sitting and listening to this man who has dedicated his life to advancing the spiritual frontiers of mankind through increased knowledge and awareness of our continuing contact with those who have gone on to a higher plane of existence, and in the light of the tremendous mass of authenticated evidence the public, and individuals have received from Fletcher, through the medium- ship of Arthur Ford, any lingering doubt in my mind about continuing life has been dispelled. If you have ever ex- perienced anything like my association with "Louie," no ex- planation is necessary. If you have not, and wouldn't believe it if it did happen, no explanation is possible.

The dead are invisible but not absent. I thank my friend Louie for making it possible for me to write this story, as far as we've taken you.

"Dad Lives in the Tree!"

Some mighty fascinating stories and accounts of actual present-day occurrences have come to light since I began my ghostly quest. Some of the things that are happening *now* are even more fascinating than the stories handed down from the past. Nothing so strange has surfaced than what is occuring right now to a family in the San Fernando Valley, right outside teeming Los Angeles. Quite recently I was allowed to sit in with this family—the strangest and most delightful group of individuals, comprised of both living and dead, that it has been my pleasure to encounter!

A mutual friend told me of the family—the mother, a girl, and two boys. The husband has been physically deceased for over a year. There is nothing strange about this, it happens all the time . . . people dying that is. What places this case out of the ordinary is the fact that father is still around—is present in and around the house—and is on a first-hand communication basis with each member of his family. Fact: father can be handled!

After hearing the foregoing sketchy details nothing would do but I must meet the visitees, pronto, and see and experience for myself, if possible. This would be one whale of a story if I could get it. Arrangements were made and you just know I was present right on time. The one thing denied me was the use of my invaluable tape recorder, so I will take you step-by-step through the progression of events as clearly as I remember them. Notes taken at the time help, and immediately upon my return home I sat down and wrote up everything concerning the, as I call it, session.

Marian, the mother, isn't just some powder-puff, chucklehead housewife. She is a teacher, an associate professor of history at a local college. The three children are most knowledgeable and articulate. The father, John, had been a practicing psychologist, well regarded in the community.

Upon meeting the family and being ushered in, I was invited to be seated in the front room of a six-room, modish, well-appointed home. Coffee was served. For my own interest, and that of astrology buffs, the first thing I asked was to know the birth dates of each. They all knew their own zodiac sign. Marian is a Libran; Carline, the daughter, twelve, is an Aries; Lyle, ten, is a Virgo; Dink, eight, is an Aquarian; deceased dad, John, was (is!) a Capricorn.

It is well-known that psychic ability does run in families, is handed down from generation to generation, and this family has it, all of them. Marian began by reading my palm, "just to see what my life and I were like." Her rendition read like my own astrological chart. Each of the kids, in turn, gave me a rundown on their own aspects, taken both from astrology and their knowledge of palmistry.

Getting down to cases, I reiterated what my friend had already told them, my prime mission of getting their story for inclusion in the book. Naturally I addressed myself primarily to Marian. "I understand John is supposed to still be here, that you and the children have conversations with him?"

"That's right. He showed up about three months after he went on. We don't have voice communication with him, yet."

"How did he show up?"

"All of us have believed in continuing life for years. We used the Ouija board to communicate with those on the other side, got word from relatives and friends who've gone on. John and I had it arranged that whichever one went first would try to communicate with the rest of us. So, we began using the board, and John did come through. He told us one time that he could be present in the house, that he would manifest the best way he could, and we would know it was him."

"When was the first time you felt his presence?"

"Oh, about seven or eight months after he left."

"How did he manifest?"

"Lyle, there, came running in from the backyard one afternoon, saying there was a ball of real cold air around the base of that tree out there, where he was playing. He said it moved with him, followed him. I thought he was just kidding me and told him to go get it, bring it in the house. Well, he did! He came in the kitchen, and said, 'Here it, is, Mother.' I walked over and felt the space in the air where he had his hands. It was very cold. It was like a ball of cold. I guess you would have to call it air, because there was nothing solid, just cold air, and it had an outline I could feel, rather irregular, not a true sphere."

"Did you at any time have any communication with that ball of cold?"

"No, not right then. When the other kids came home, we got the Ouija board out and tried a sitting. It worked. John came through and said that the ball of cold air was his way of manifesting, that it was the only way he could do it now, that he was working on other methods of materializing, and for us to keep trying to make contact. He did suggest we use a method of communicating he had worked out about five years ago."

Carline ran to the hall closet and got out a box. She spread cut-out letters of the alphabet on the coffee table in a semi-circle, turned a light, glass tumbler upside down for use as the planchette. The rest of us seated ourselves before the table, and Carline placed the fingers of her right hand lightly on top of the glass. We sat quietly for a moment as they "tuned in," as they put it. Then Carline asked if someone was present in the room with us? The glass, with just the tips of her fingers touching it, shot over to the word YES, on the table. She asked who—in rapid succession, the glass quickly moved to the letters JOHN, then DAD. I wrote down what was coming through.

I've had enough experience with this type of communication that I couldn't be convinced until I'd tried it myself. They allowed me to sit in Carline's place, place my own hand on the glass, ask my own questions. No sooner had I touched the glass with the tips of my fingers, than it practically jumped away from me to spell out the word HELLO. I asked for his last name and it came, so quickly I had difficulty keeping my fingers on the glass. The family last name was spelled out without mistake. My next question was, "Do you know why I am here?" The glass shot over to YES. I asked "Do you mind?" The glass shot over to NO. Then it continued, "Go to the hall." I looked at Marian. Dink said, "I'll take you. Dad likes to stay near the heater when he's in the house." I arose and followed him into the hall, in full view of those in the room. The heater is an outlet in the wall, at floor height. Dink put out his hands as though feeling for something in mid air. "Here he is." I put my hands out to the spot, and by golly there was only what I can describe as a "ball" of very cold air. The moment I touched it, chills shot up and down my arms, my hair seemed to stand on end. When I took my hands away from it, the chills left. I touched the "ball" a number of times. It wasn't visible, just there. It didn't move, and I could pass my hands through it. To me it felt elliptical, like a football, only larger.

Dink and I went back to the coffee table and sat down in front of the letters. I placed my hand on the glass again, and asked, "How do I know it is you, John?" The glass immediately spelled out BELIEVE; then the glass moved on to "GO TO THE TREE." Lyle spoke up and said, "That's where dad lives." All of us got up and went into the back yard, to the only tree, an orange, about twenty-five feet high. The kids started feeling about in the air, and Carline found him first. "Here he is."

I walked over and put my hands where she had hers. There was that ball of very cold air. The chills shot up and down my arms as I passed my hands through and around it, outlined it, as it were. There was no spoken word, no materialization, just the ball of air. Then it wasn't there. Carline said, "I bet he's gone back inside." We then trooped back to the table, sat down, and they insisted I work the glass. The moment I put my fingers on it, it began to move. YOU KNOW ONLY A LITTLE. MORE WILL COME LATER. That was all. Then the glass refused to move, even when the kids and Marian tried it.

Next they showed me two small articles, a classroom eraser, and a ball-point pen which John is supposed to have apported from the classroom where Marian teaches to the house and dropped on the kitchen table while they were eating dinner about two months ago. Nothing of the sort happened while I was present, and I had to accept their word for it.

By this time I'd been there for a little over two hours, and not wanting to overstay my leave, with an eye to the future and additional evidence and/or communication with John, I excused myself, thanked them all heartily, and departed.

It seems here that John has applied himself diligently to finding methods for a type of materialization and of communicating with the family—of actually remaining present about the house and property so that he can be in contact, and be contacted at all times.

If you will remember, it has been observed that ectoplasm can be invisible vapor. It doesn't seem that John, materializing ectoplasmically, needs to draw on the vital force of any of the family. They also reported they didn't feel chills until they touched the ball of air. From the extensive written material on the subject, it might just be it isn't actually good for the family or beneficial to himself for John to stay around so long and concern himself so intimately with the earthly life of his family. Rather, it is posited that the excarnate, although still retaining love, thought, and devotion to the ones left behind, apply himself to his own progression, ready himself for that plateau, and the next.

This is my personal observation based on reading and discussions with leading mediums who've dealt with the "other side" for many years. Who knows what the mission of any spirit is once he's gone on? It could be that John is doing what he is doing to bring more knowledge and understanding to the living. Perhaps one of the three children will devote his life to the study of psychic phenomena, which will help bring to light more of the knowledge mankind seeks.

There will be other sessions with these interesting people and with many others like them. I shall hope to be embarked on writing another book by then, which I will entitle *More Great Ghosts of the West.*

"Tilt the Table, Patsy"

That's what we walked into the night we visited a woman and her daughter who were reputed to be table tilters. They should also be called table walkers, because the table *did* waddle across the floor, lift three legs off the floor and dip one of the legs into a glass of champagne! Having her evening drink, was the way Mrs. Pauline Byrne and her daughter Mary Ann put it. But we're ahead of the story. Let's go back and come in again, at the beginning.

I'd heard about the Byrnes from some friends of mine. They enthused about how they had this ghost of some girl who'd died quite awhile ago, had her right there in the house, and quite frequently, Mrs. Byrne and Mary Ann would sit down at this card table, with or without others present, and they would have a "conversation" with Patsy, the discarnate entity who communicated with them through the medium of the table.

Actually, I am credulously incredulous. I believe, please help me in my unbelief. My friends arranged the meeting, and at the appointed hour, my wife, Florence, Dr. Freda Morris, Ph.D, a parapsychology researcher, Joseph Agnello, TV director, and I knocked at the door of the Byrne house in

Northridge, California. We were admitted by Mr. Byrne, who took our coats. He eyed the portable tape recorder I'd brought along but made no comment or move to divest me of it.

There were five people seated around the flimsy card table in the Byrne's front room. That's normal . . . sitting around a card table. The date was Tuesday, March 17, 1970. What wasn't normal was the way the table was acting! It was raising two legs off the floor, then either lowering them gently to the carpeted floor, or bringing them down with quite an audible thump, then rising again, to repeat the process.

We new guests seated ourselves on the couch, and just watched, but only for a moment. Questions were being asked the "table" and it was replying with Yes or No answers. Two raps on the floor for Yes, one rap for No; when it didn't know the answer, or refused to answer, it remained quiet. This was too much for me, and I grabbed the tape recorder and scooted over to the corner of the table where sat a woman whom I felt must be Mrs. Byrne. She was having a ball and seemed in command of the situation. She was repeating questions asked by the others seated around the table, and addressing someone named Patsy.

"Patsy, the question is, . . . will it happen?"

The table would rise on two legs (and it didn't matter *which* two legs; east, west, south, or north) then descend with one or two thumps on the floor. The woman turned to me, extended one hand, smiled and said, "I'm Pauline Byrne," then indicated a lovely young girl on her right. "This is my daughter, Mary Ann."

I introduced myself hurriedly, not wanting to disrupt whatever was going on. During this introduction time, I noted the table rise again, and come down, hard, once. Mrs.

Byrne looked at the guests, laughing, "That was a *definite* No."

Immediately I looked at the woman sitting behind the side of the table which had remained on the floor. She had both hands resting on it, so I figured she couldn't be pulling it down with her knees, unless she was wired to it, or had suction cups on her legs. I quickly introduced Florence, Dr. Morris, and Joe Agnello to Mrs. Byrne, and she introduced them to the sitters around the table. Everyone took their hands off the table, acknowledged the introductions, and chatted among themselves.

"Mrs. Byrne, I'm new at this table tilting thing, would you mind if I used the tape recorder?"

"No, go ahead, I don't think Patsy minds—do you Patsy?"

She still had one hand resting on the table. It rose on two legs and came down with a moderate thump on the carpet.

"No, she doesn't mind, although she went after one man who brought a tape recorder. She didn't like him. Do you like this man, Patsy?"

The table rose and descended twice. Thump, Thump. "Yes, she likes you."

"Thank you, Patsy," I said, hoping to sound like a man who had been talking to tables for a long time, or even manipulating them myself; sound sophisticated, that's it.

My wife and Dr. Morris couldn't stand it any longer and they came to the table. Room was made for them. Joe Agnello remained seated on the couch; he'd seen table tilting done before. Old hat! Now there were seven people seated around the table, actively participating in playing Tilt the Table. I wanted to remain free to roam, snoop, stoop, check, pry. A half dozen questions later, Mrs. Byrne asked me if I would like to ask a question? I did. Addressing the table, much like a golfer addressing the ball, I inquired, "Will my book be a success, Patsy?" (I was getting familiar.)

Immediately the two legs rose and descended in a rapid two-thump Yes.

"When will it be published?"

One thump. I looked questioningly at Mrs. Byrne. "No?"

After further questioning, Patsy made it clear that she meant the year 1971. "Is that right Patsy, 1971?"

Two thumps on the carpet. "Thank you, Patsy."

"Mrs. Byrne, how can you tell the difference between the answer No and the first letter of the alphabet?" I asked.

"We had to devise a method of communicating without going clear through the alphabet to spell out each word. She gives the first letter of the word, then we sort of play a guessing game as to what it might be."

I turned to Patsy, I mean the table, and asked, "Patsy, what are the initials of the literary agent who is handling my book?"

There were two quick thumps on the carpet. "That is *b*," said Mrs. Byrne.

The table rose and descended quickly, thump, thump, thump, eleven times.

"That is *k*," from Mrs. Myrne. "b, k. Is that right?" she looked at me.

"Bertha Klausner, that's right. Where is she, Patsy?"

Again that rapid thumping—*n*, and then *y*. "That must be New York," supplied Mrs. Byrne.

I asked the question "Is it New York, Patsy?" Two thumps, Yes.

With that, Mrs. Byrne rose from her chair, stretched, and said they would continue the session after the coffee and sandwich break.

"Mrs. Byrne," I asked, "when you break off contact like this, break the communication, can you just pick it up again?"

"Oh, sure. Patsy is here most of the time. When she's feeling good we've been able to go practically all night. Sometimes I've had to quit because I was just exhausted, Mary Ann and I both, and we've gone to bed. The next morning when we sit down to breakfast, Patsy comes through and we have a brisk conversation."

"Do you know who Patsy was, in life, I mean?' How old she was?"

"Oh, yes. She told us she lived in England during the Irish-English Revolution, that she'd been shot in front of a post office in London, by an Irishman. She was nineteen."

"Did she tell you who her family was? Was she married?"

"We know who her family was, and who her relatives are, but she doesn't want us to contact them. They wouldn't believe it, and it would make them unhappy. She wasn't married, no."

Luckily, Mrs. Byrne wasn't hesitant about answering questions. She and her daughter thoroughly enjoy their contact with Patsy and the attention it's focused on them from such groups as scientists, doctors, clergy, psychiatrists, spiritualists, writers, physicists, psychologists, and parapsychologists.

"Have you been scientifically checked out, you and Mary Ann? I mean have you, Mary Ann, and the table been scientifically instrumented?"

She laughed. "We've been so instrumented at times we thought we were walking electrical gadgets! They've hooked electrodes all over us, had us dress in hospital gowns. You name it, they've done it."

Now Dr. Morris took over for some questions, and we will have to be circumspect in the use of names because it might be embarrassing to the individual, and we could be sued!

"Didn't you appear on a local TV show, not too long ago?"

"Oh, yes, we had a lot of fun. Patsy was in great shape. She didn't want to quit."

"What was the opinion of those on the show, the people in the studio?"

"They thought it was a great show, but some of them thought we were frauds. One man hollered at me from the audience that I should be put in jail!"

"What conclusions have the scientists come to, about this phenomenon?"

"Let me talk about just one, a professor. He came out and watched one night. He asked us to do a certain thing. Patsy refused. Even though Patsy had answered a lot of questions he asked, when she refused to do the test he wanted, he got in a huff, said the whole thing didn't make sense, and he packed up and left. Patsy didn't like him anyhow."

We sat for awhile, drinking coffee and eating the sandwiches, listening to the conversation from the others. It was the first time I'd been involved with table tilting, and I was truly amazed at what I was seeing. It's also most interesting to note how quickly people adjust to something new. A few questions to others in the room elicited the fact that two of them had never sat in on a table tilt session, and yet, here they were, allegedly in the presence of a discarnate entity, which most everyone would call a ghost, named Patsy, chatting away as though it was something they did every day. We were all alert, charged up, but pretty thoroughly believing, and comfortable in the belief, that we were communicating with a dead person! I personally felt that Patsy was another living, breathing, present human being.

The coffee klatch was over. Mrs. Byrne bid everyone who wished to return to the table and we would get back in touch with Patsy. Florence and Dr. Morris quickly took their places at the table, while I resumed my prowling with the tape recorder, trying to get the questions as they were asked. It was difficult. If you've tried to tape-record a group of people who are all talking at once, making side remarks, laughing, you know what I was up against.

When everyone was seated, they all placed their hands on the table. Mrs. Byrne said, "Patsy, we're back, let's go to work. Table rise."

In just seconds, the table did just that. It reared back, two legs on the floor, two legs suspended about a foot off the floor.

Just for the fun of it, and I know you are wondering at this point, set up a bridge table, either a flimsy one or the heavier type. Seat yourself, and then, by merely placing your hands flat on the table, try to make it tilt without showing any indication you are manipulating it. Try to make it tilt to your left, right. Or, have someone else do it, and observe how any physical motion they make which would move the table in the slightest is quite obvious. Mrs. Byrne and Mary Ann wore dresses without sleeves, bare to the shoulders. Mrs. Byrne was seated, this time, on the east side of the table, Mary Ann on the west side, and the table would tilt sometimes north, sometimes south. There were times when each woman only had one hand, each, on the table when it tilted and answered questions. Now you try it. (You might even find you *can* do it, that you have the gift of table tilting!)

Back to Patsy's table. Patsy was asked if she would like to have her nightly drink? Two emphatic thumps—Yes!

"What would you like to have?" asked Mrs. Byrne.

Quickly, three thumps. "*a* ... *b* ... *c*. Coke?" A no thump.

"Crown Cola?" They were playing games with her, and she undoubtedly knew it. A no thump.

I said, "Champagne?" Two yes staccato thumps. Everyone laughed.

Mr. Byrne had already gone to the kitchen, and now he returned with a stemmed glass and a bottle of the bubbly. He poured the glass half-full, placed it off the rug, on the plastic-covered floor. Now everyone rose. They cleared the area between the table and the glass, a distance of some eight feet. Five people had their hands resting on the table. Mrs. Byrne and Mary Ann each had only one hand resting on it, palms down.

"All right, sweetheart, go get your drink. Come on, Patsy, there it is."

The table began to rock from side to side. Then it began a definite forward motion, rocking itself along, inching along would be more apt. I got down on all fours, microphone in hand, and tried my best to see if anyone was pushing the table or kicking the legs with their feet. Nothing. Dr. Morris and Florence had their eyeballs run out on little stems! Even Joe Agnello had risen from his place on the couch. This he had never seen. Finally the table reached the glass. Now came the topper. While I watched each participant carefully, the table tilted back until it had three legs off the floor, slowly it swung around and over, one leg hovering directly above the glass. The leg descended downward, made a gentle pass at it and missed. It rose again, then lowered. All the while both Mrs. Byrne and Mary Ann were urging Patsy on.

"A little bit to your left, Patsy. No, no, too far. Back to your right. Now, darling, now."

The one leg, directly over the glass, descended slowly into the glass and rested there for a moment. People were laughing, talking, bending to see, then the glass tipped over and the champagne spilled out on the floor.

"That's why I don't like to use my good, stemmed glasses; sometimes she breaks them," said Mrs. Byrne. "All right, now you've spilled your drink. Make pictures in the champagne."

The leg swung up and over, descended into the spilled liquid, and began making circular motions. Mrs. Byrne and Mary Ann still had only one hand, each, on the table. I saw Dr. Morris watching the other participants for any sign they might be assisting the table. We looked at each other. I elevated my eyebrows, she elevated her eyebrows and shrugged. This highly trained doctor of psychology, and a parapsychologist, a woman who had spent many years researching phenomena, writing up scientific hypotheses postulating suppositions and conclusions was as amazed by what was going on as I was. I heard my wife, Florence, say a number of times, "This is the most amazing thing I ever saw!"

As if right on cue, when we thought we'd witnessed the peak scene in the play, there was a knock on the front door. A young man, a neighbor, was admitted. He advanced into the hallway, was introduced all around, then, noting the table standing in the puddle of grape, asked what was going on.

"Patsy tried to take a drink of champagne, and she spilled it."

"Who is Patsy?"

"She's the one who contacts us through the table. She tilts it."

He folded his arms over his chest, which indicated he closed right up. "I don't believe it."

Mrs. Byrne was the only one touching the table now. She had one hand on it.

"Patsy, he doesn't believe it. What do you say to that?" The table rose on its two, shall I say, hind legs, and hung there, motionless.

"Why don't you go over and hit him, Patsy?"

"This I gotta see," said the young man. He planted himself. I turned up the tape recorder, louder. I didn't want to miss a thing. A performance like this might never again be duplicated, for me! (Are you still with me?)

Patsy-the-Table walked over and gave the young man two hard hits on the leg! He jumped back, pointed at the table, not at Mrs. Byrne, and said, "Knock that crap off!"

That is like the man who shook his clenched fist heavenward and shouted he didn't believe in God! With that, Patsy (and you see how convinced *I* was) reared back for another onslaught. The young man retreated, still saying he didn't believe it. He left, shortly, and I'm sure he has had time to talk to himself. "Self," he has probably said, "were you or were you not attacked by a table called Patsy?"

It was now growing late. I believed the only way the last two performances could be topped would be if Patsy-the-Table walked out the front door, got into a car, and drove away. It seemed we had been talking with and watching Patsy for hours. How do you say thank you and goodbye to a ghost? We made our amenities to Mrs. Byrne, Mary Ann, Mr. Byrne, and the other guests, then asked Mrs. Byrne to thank Patsy and tell her goodbye.

"Why don't you do it yourself?"

"Ok."

Mrs. Byrne once again placed her hand on the table. I said, "Goodbye, Patsy, and thank you so much."

Immediately the table tilted back, and in rapid succession, using the alphabet, counted out the letters *bye,* then settled back on the floor.

We left.

The question no doubt occurred to you as to whether any other discarnates ever came through the table, ever operated it. When asked, Mrs. Byrne said that there had been three or four other entities, yes. One had been a Hindu girl. When messages from her were spelled out, the Byrnes had to call the local libraries and talk with the foreign language people to get the messages interpreted. The messages were in English as well as Hindu.

Table tilting has been known since the invention of tables. Science has termed this type of manifestation either telekinesis or psychokinesis. Telekinesis is the movement of an object caused while not in contact with the body generating the force, and is supposedly caused by spiritistic methods. The body generating the force in this case was Mrs. Byrne and Mary Ann. Apparently, Patsy hasn't the ability, or hasn't progressed far enough to be able to do the moving herself. Some would term it psychokinesis—the strange effects of mind on matter. An excellent example of psychokinesis is the reknowned Ted Serios. His thoughtographs, projections of his mental images onto (or into) film or a photographic plate are well known. (See *The World of Ted Serios,* by Dr. Jules Eisenbud.)

Pranksters and Things

The
House Haunter

House haunting is one of the most interesting of the phenomena, perhaps because it is such a personal thing. Having
someone in the house whom you can see is one thing, but
having a guest or visitor you know is present and you can't
see gets a little hairy.

There is such a visitor in Bridgeport, California. Of course,
if you want to be fair about it, he does have prior rights; he
built the house about one hundred years ago, and, as in the
case in the TV series "The Ghost And Mrs. Muir," the house
still belongs to him.

The question could be posed as to whether the ghost is a
"new" one or the "old" one who has been around so many
years. Ghosts, like their physically evident counterparts walking about in visible form, have certain patterns—*modus
operandi,* the police call it—that identifies them. This house
ghost hasn't changed its *modus operandi.* I believe that what
we are about to encounter in the following haunting shows
what is called *retrocognition:* a memory of the past, rather
than any knowledge of the present occupants, or even a
caring about them.

Mrs. Grace Branden, a long-time resident of Bridgeport, isn't a person given to hallucinations, is highly regarded as a solid citizen, and has worked for some of the most reputable county and state officials as well as being a businesswoman in her own right. Mrs. Branden began at the beginning and brought me up to date.

In the 1880s, an industrious resident of Bridgeport, A.P. Allen, built a house on the main street of town. It is a splendid product of the period, being a large, two-story frame dwelling, solidly built, outlined with the gingerbread con-figurations in vogue at the time. Not much is remembered or even known about the personal life of A.P. Allen, except that he was in business, did very well at it. His house was one of the better homes in Bridgeport, and is one of the few older ones still standing in good condition.

Sometime after Mr. Allen built the house, and moved the family in, he, for some unknown reason, committed suicide in one of the two upstairs bedrooms. Years later the Brandens bought the house, and Grace was given the bed-room that they found out later, was the one in which Allen had taken his life.

Let Grace take it: "I lived there many years ago. We had not heard from anyone at that time about the place being haunted. Maybe it wasn't until we moved in. The first time anything happened was when a girl friend was staying with me one night. We were awakened by the bedclothes being pulled off us. I thought at first it was my friend doing the pulling, and she thought I was doing it, and we both pulled on the blankets. They were pulled right away from us, right out of our hands, pulled clear off the bed and dropped out in the middle of the floor!"

Grace called to her mother who was sleeping in the other upstairs bedroom. When the girls explained what had happened, the mother naturally assumed the two teen-agers were having a little fun, or had been dreaming. She tucked them in snuggly, and told them to stop their nonsense.

"We went back to sleep, finally, and I don't know how long it was, but we both woke up again and the bedclothes were being pulled off the bed. Somebody was doing it and it wasn't us. We watched the blankets move across the bed, slide off onto the floor and then pile into a heap in the middle of the floor. From what we could see, they looked as though they were being pulled by someone or something, like a person would do it. There was enough light in the room to see there was no one there but us. We were so scared we wouldn't sleep in the room anymore, and my mother let us sleep in bed with her, in the other room."

If the ghost were an angry one it seemingly would do a lot more than just pull the bedclothes off people. It has an excellent chance of doing bodily harm if it can pick up objects, but it has never exhibited physical violence, although, as Grace says, bedclothes being pulled off you is pretty violent!

"Many times, for some years actually, when we would all be downstairs, we would hear the bedsprings creak, someone putting their feet on the floor, getting up and walking, shuffling across the room, sort of pacing back and forth. But we've never seen anyone when we would all go up to investigate."

It made no difference whether it was summer, spring, or winter; if the weather was balmy, rainy or cold and snowing, the sounds from that upstairs bedroom were, and are, always the same.

"We finally sold the house. This is a small town and you hear most of what is happening with people. The people who bought the house rented out that bedroom, sometimes the whole upper floor, during the summer months when so many tourists and fishermen come up here. There have been a number of people stay in the room, and most of them have moved out after a night or two, usually after the first night. They are scared of what is going on in there, the bedclothes being pulled off them, someone pacing around the room. One young lady got up in the middle of the night and moved right out. She said she couldn't stand the 'haunting.' That ghost, if it is Mr. Allen, has never spoken to anyone; it just goes about its own business, doing the same thing, year after year."

The house is presently leased to a Los Angeles superior court judge, who had his law practice in Bridgeport when he was a young barrister. I met him twenty years ago when I was appearing in a movie *Out of the Past,* starring Robert Mitchum. It was made in Bridgeport and various sections of the surrounding High Sierras. The judge spends the summers in the house. It would seem he is fully aware, he and his family, of the ghost, but for some reason they aren't particularly bothered by it. They live in a haunted house and seem to like it! Or just don't care! Or, maybe they don't believe in ghosts and pay no attention when the bedclothes are pulled off them, or when someone who isn't visible gets up and paces around the room.

The haunting has been going for over fifty years. If the ghost is Mr. Allen, either he doesn't know he can leave, move on; or, because of the nature of his death by suicide, he is now chained to the place where he took his life.

The
Lunch Bucket

The following story was told to me by Lee Symonds, Mono County historian, and curator of the Bridgeport Museum, Bridgeport, California, September 14, 1969. I took the picture of Lee holding the lunch bucket, knife, fork, and spoon found in the tunnel. I will leave this in Lee's personal narrative.

"In 1960 three men friends and I went on a deer hunt. We were going into the Monte Cristo area, about forty miles from Bridgeport. We had to go through a gate on the way, so Charles got one key. When we got to the junction of the road where the gate was, we found the key wouldn't work. We decided to go back up to the top of the hill and take a little track we saw leading up into the pinon trees.

"Charles was driving, the rest of us were watching for deer. We didn't pay any attention to where we were going. Finally Charles said, 'What kind of a road am I on?' We looked, and the jeep was on the trail, but there were tracks leading off in another direction, as far as we could see. It was a wagon road. We took a vote and decided to take the old road. The farther we went the better the road became. The sun had just set. We could see a rock shelf up above us, about five hundred feet from us at that time. When we topped out on that shelf under a big pine tree we were right in the street of what was later to be, we found out, Boulder Flat. Above Boulder Flat was the old town of Bellefort. We didn't find out the names until three years later. No one knew of this place. I tell you this so you will know how old the place was. When we found this town, no, we refound it, none of the old-timers in this area knew anything about it. I discovered the name of Boulder Flat from an old-timer in Ely, Nevada, who had helped build the road we came upon. He said, 'Yes, that's Boulder Flat. There was also an old ghost town up there called Kaintuck.'

"Leading out of Boulder Flat was a road that wound up the side of the mountain, and at this time we were at the 10,225 feet elevation. We took the road, and it disappeared around the shoulder of the mountain. We decided the next morning we would drive up and see where it went, because from there we could get an even better panoramic view than where we were, which was already fabulous. The little road wound around the side of the mountain and ended at a tunnel, which was the main mine for the town of Boulder Flat. It was the MT tunnel, a relocation of the Ford claim, and later it was known as the Fredericks Mine. Ann Webb, the county clerk in Bridgeport, is Frederick's descendant four generations removed.

"It was a very narrow mine tunnel, and it wasn't very high. It took a small man to get in there and stand up. All those miners back then must have been little squirts. The strata of the vein leaned to the left, where the vein matter had deposited between the upper wall and the lower, called the hanging wall, and the foot wall. If a man was standing up his head would almost hit the corner of the hanging wall. It had little rails to carry the ore cars. The mine car was still sitting the rail, outside, and it worked, because I took a ride on it and almost went over the dump, down the canyon. The others wanted to go into the tunnel but I was a little bit hesitant because old mines are dangerous. You never know when they will cave in, even if they never have, they might decide this is the day they will!

"The others went ahead. I took pictures of them as they went in. I was the last one to go in. We all had lights with us, and used them to see where we were going. It was interesting to see that there were stalactites and stalagmites, formed of ice, beautiful things. They seemed to be a procession of ghosts walking down into the shaft. Some were two or three feet high. The narrow gauge mine tracks are only about two feet apart, very narrow. You couldn't walk anywhere but in the center of the tracks. We tried to get some pictures in the shaft, we didn't know how well we'd done getting them. We found some old tools, some old picks, made as they did in those days, hand made. We found a couple of old miner's shoes. I have them in the museum.

"It was quite cold in there and we decided we had a lot of looking around to do outside, so we all came back out. We'd gone about two hundred feet into the shaft. So we all came back out, right in the center of the narrow gauge rails, single file. We went back down to our camp, went deer hunting, looked around the old town. That evening Don said, 'Let's go back to the tunnel, I found some larger power flashbulbs in my suitcase.' He wanted to take more pictures of the ice formations.

"The next morning we drove back up and walked in the mine shaft, went down about fifty feet, just the two of us, this time. Don was ahead of me. I shined my light on the tracks, as he was also doing, to see where we were going and looking for anything we could take back with us. We took some pictures and then started back out of the tunnel. Don was ahead of me on the way out, about five feet. About thirty feet from the opening of the tunnel, there, in between the rails, close to the left rail, but sitting oblong to the rail, was a lunch bucket. It had a knife, fork, and spoon in it. It didn't have a lid, but it had a wooden handle. The day before when we were in there, every one of us had gone into the tunnel, way beyond where this bucket was found, then came out. This day Don and I had gone into the tunnel, beyond where we found the bucket, and on the way out, found it.

"I picked it up and called to Don. He came back and we looked it over with our lights. It is damp, muddy in the tunnel. The dirt in the middle of the tracks is mud, you could see your footprints. I turned the bucket over and noted it was dry on the bottom. I asked Don if he had put it there and he said that he hadn't. We looked at the walls of the tunnel, and there was no shelf where it could have fallen from.

"While we were looking at it I was hit with a tremendous chill. I looked at Don, and he said, 'Do you feel that?' I said I was having awful chills. They ran up and down my back, and that's what Don said he was having. The wind wasn't blowing in the mine tunnel. It never blows that far back in any tunnel I've ever been in. It was cold in the tunnel, but this was something else, it was a physical cold, like someone throwing buckets of cold air on our bodies under our clothes.

"We went outside and the chills continued until we'd gotten in the Jeep and gone about halfway back to the camp. When we told the others they laughed at us and said one of us was playing a joke on the other. They didn't remember seeing the bucket, or any other obstruction in between the rails when they went into the tunnel, or came out.

"I can't explain what happened, but I do know that bucket wasn't there until Don and I started walking out, and how he missed either stepping on it, or seeing it with his bright flashlight, I don't know. How could four men, with bright lamps shining on the ground at their feet, looking for possible artifacts or objects, have missed that lunch bucket? And how come it wasn't even damp on the bottom, sitting right on the wet, muddy dirt?

"I wish that whoever, or whatever, put that bucket there, if they were a ghost, could have given us some better evidence than those chills and the bucket. That's all. I have the bucket here in the museum, the one you took the picture of. We all feel that it was put there by someone who's been dead a long time, and they were trying to get in touch with us, let us know they are around. I hope they're not all alone."

To the above can be added a partial explanation of the phenomena. It is called *apporting,* the movement of an object from one place to another with no visible means of its conveyance, or support, through locked doors, walls, and over long distances, with no apparent damage or disturbance of the object moved.

Why
the Bedclothes?

In our story of "The House Haunter," we dealt with the ghost of A.P. Allen who pulled the bedclothes off the two young girls and dumped them in the middle of the floor. I've heard many stories of bedclothes pullers around the country, and finally it has happened to me!

During the week of October 24-29, 1969, I was employed by MGM Studios, Culver City, California, to play a role in a segment of the "Then Came Bronson" TV series. The picture was made on location in Mesa, Arizona. We stayed at the Velda Rose Motel, a huge complex catering to retired people. The second night we were there I had gone to bed about 10:30 P.M., and had just dozed off enough to be in that in-between land of sleep and distant wakefulness. That plateau, by the way, is the best time for psychic phenomena to occur. I was lying on my right side, my head on the pillow.

Suddenly the pillow felt as though it was being withdrawn, backwards, from under my head, enough so that my faculties came awake and jumped to icy attention! I laid there for a moment, just feeling, waiting. The pillow was little by little definitely being pulled away. Slowly I ran my hand up the sheet, grasped the pillow, held onto it. It didn't move anymore. Then I let go of it, and without moving my body, waited.

In seconds it began to move again! I'd not shaved since early morning, and as the material of the pillow was drawn across my whiskers they made a distinct scratching sound. No, I was not moving my head, my body wasn't moving . . . the pillow was being moved. Only then did I finally turn my head and try, by the light coming in from outside, to see if there was something or someone present having some fun with me. Nothing. I turned over and snapped on the table lamp on the bedstand and looked around the room. Nothing.

Naturally, I looked at the pillow. It was about six inches from where my head would have been resting on it had I been lying down. Turning off the light, I assumed the same position and waited. It didn't happen again, there was no movement of the pillow or other bedclothes. Next thing I knew the telephone was stridently demanding I get up and get moving for the day's filming.

I recounted the story on the set that day, and a young actress in the company from Hollywood seemed quite agitated at it. She kept coming to me during the day and asking if it couldn't have been "something else," that I didn't *really* have that happen to me? The following morning she sheepishly admitted it had scared her so much she slept down at the foot of the bed, wouldn't use the pillow, in the hope my pillow puller wouldn't get into her room and try the same thing! No one else in the company reported any strange happenings during the rest of our stay, and their attitude about my episode was one of half-believing, half-derison, like, "Had any spooks lately?!"

Since man began reaching into deep space searching for life on other planets by use of long wave radio, his attempts have been rewarded by receiving radio signals at about nine hundred megacycles. Evidently, those signals have been broadcasting for quite some time, we have only just begun to tune into them. If we mortals go on from this physical life into a cosmic life, then we may try to make contact from wherever we find ourselves. Not all of us are scientists, can't figure out intricate and involved laboratory methods of some kind of contact, so, perhaps the majority of us have to be satisfied, on the other side, with letting those here know of our presence by pulling bedclothes, throwing pots, pans, and shoes around a room. And that's the way much of the phenomena occur, subtly, quietly, almost delicately. But they do happen. It's for us to recognize that we are *spirits,* being contacted by other *spirits* by methods which most times leave much to be desired in establishing recognizable contact.

This manifestation has nothing to do with Ghosts of California, but it had something to do with me! Maybe it was my friend, Louie?

Marv,
the Furniture Mover

Let's take a look at the movement of objects heavier than bedclothes by the excarnates!

Arthur and Anne Webb (no relation to me) are residents of Bridgeport, California. A great many stories of all types come from that huge town of five hundred population. Well, that's Bridgeport, three hundred and fifty miles north of Los Angeles, on Highway 395. It is steeped in well-deserved tradition and legend. The people who went into that area, including nearby Bodie, weren't exactly armchair pioneers. Anne is a lifelong resident of the area, and has been employed in the Mono County Courthouse for many years. Arthur wasn't born there, so he comes under the heading of accepted outsiders. This is the way Anne's story went, handed down to her from her grandmother. It took place in the late 1890s.

Forty-two miles out of Bridgeport, is a place known as Smith Valley, given over primarily to cattle ranching, along with the growing of sufficient feed during the summer months to see the cattle through the extremely rugged winters. The ranch where the incidents occurred belonged to Anne's grandmother. They had about six young, unmarried cowhands to run the place. The cowboys were quartered on the ground floor of a large two-story bunkhouse. The second floor was a sort of dayroom for the hands to relax in during evenings and weekends. One of the young men was named Marvin, who had worked at the ranch for some four or five years. As is the habit and custom of young men who live in those remote areas, about once or twice a month they would ride into town to take care of personal business, and have a few hours of drinking and small talk at a local saloon. On one of the trips Marvin took to a town called Mountain House, he got into a fracas with another cowboy over the attentions of one of the bar belles, was waylaid when he rode out of town on his homeward trip, and murdered. When they heard about it, his bunkmates rode into Mountain House, but the assailant had removed himself to parts unknown. His friends claimed the body, and returned Marvin to the Smith Valley Ranch. In those days, and in some remote areas today, it wasn't unusual for a ranch to have its own graveyard, where members of the family and the cowboys were buried. They buried Marv there on the ranch, about a half mile from the main house.

Marv had been a favorite with everyone at the ranch, and his passing depressed them for quite awhile. It was a few weeks later, according to Anne, before the cowboys felt like indulging in any games or sport around the bunkhouse, but they decided to have a poker session upstairs in their dayroom.

When they arrived in the room, they noticed that the poker table, which had always been placed in the south end of the room, had been moved to the north end. They moved it back and spent the evening playing cards. It was remarked by one of the cowboys at the time that Marvin had always tried to get them to move the table to the north end, for what reason no one seemed to know.

Two nights later the boys again had a poker session, and it was again noted when they entered the room, the table was moved from the south to the north end. They wanted to know who the wise guy was who had moved it, and everyone denied doing it, or having any knowledge of it.

Over the next two months, each time they went into the game room the table had been moved, as they said, to where Marv wanted it, at the north end. They began to watch each other pretty closely. It seemed to them someone was having fun at the expense of Marv's memory, and they became incensed. They slept downstairs, right under the room, and never heard any noise of the table being moved, and did their own cleaning and maintenance of the quarters. Finally they got so disturbed at the occurrence, they detailed a different man each day to keep watch that none of the others entered the room during daylight hours, and when anyone did go into it, in the evening, they would all go with him.

This didn't work, either! They moved the table back each time, from the north end to the south end. The next time they went into the room it had been moved north. They even placed a ball on the floor and waited to see if it would roll. It didn't. The floor was even.

In desperation they nailed the windows shut, moved the table to its accustomed place, put a lock on the door, and gave the keys to Anne's grandmother to keep until they all wanted to go into it at once. The table would have been moved back to "where Marv wanted it" regardless of their stratagems and security measures!

That is the only manifestation they ever had that Marvin was still with them. Years later, when the ranch passed into other hands, the table was still being moved from the south to the north end of the room. None of the cowboys ever saw

Marv, or even said they saw him, or had any communicatioι from him other than the table being moved. It became known as Marv's room, and when the cowboys wanted to impress a visitor, they would all go in a group, move the table to the south end of the room, then the next day take the wide-eyed visitor up, and sure enough, the table would be back in Marv's corner.

The above is one of those telekinetic phenomenons—the movement of inanimate objects not in contact with a visible force or body, nor by spiritualistic means.

We wish we knew more about the *how* of telekinesis. Ectoplasmic exudations, the emission of pulpy, almost plastic substance from the bodies of entranced mediums has been observed and photographed moving objects by means of rods and levers by which the ectoplasm assumes to do the job. There is the story, also, of a young man who devoted himself to trying to move a ball of cotton by merely concentrating on it. He employed every protection he and a friend could devise to keep from having his breath or any errant breeze disturb it, such as sitting as far as five feet from the table holding the ball, his mouth shielded by a mask that diverted his breath out behind him. After three months of intense application, the ball was observed to move! As time went on he became more facile, and within fifteen or twenty minutes of intense concentration, the ball would move, not much, but move it did, and it was accomplished in front of critical witnesses who attested to the fact in writing.

Science tells us that all is energy, but we still don't know how the spirits of the departed operate to move objects, aside from their own explanation of using "thought," and it would seem that thought takes many forms.

He Plays
Tricks on Me

Gardnerville, Nevada, squats athwart the highway where California meets Nevada. It is at the base of the mountain road leading up to Lake Tahoe. In towns like this there are usually old-timers who are wells of stories and information about the past. They've mostly moved into town due to advancing age, their days of rugged living and mining just a memory.

I dropped into the local post office and asked the fellows on duty if there were any old-timers about from whom I might get some stories of the past? They all agreed that old Russ would be the one I was looking for. The rural mail carrier happened to be present, happened to be going out that way, and volunteered to guide me to Russ's place, up in the Sierras, on the California side.

They warned me that old Russ was a cantankerous old feller, you never knew how you would be greeted, so I sort of resigned myself to being rebuffed when I met him and brought up the subject of ghosts!

Volkswagons on steep grades in the mountains aren't the most agile of vehicles, and I loafed along behind this struggling one, ever rising to the 6,500-foot level. The highway finally graded onto an asphalt road which became real snaky. The VW turned off to one side and my guide alighted and beckoned me to follow. The day was windy, and at 6,500 feet, the lowering clouds presaged snow rather than rain at this altitude and time of year.

The house, as we approached it, looked saggy. The front, with no porch, appeared like the desolate face of a halloween pumpkin about two weeks after it had been carved . . . kinda shriveling, lined and seamed with age. But not so with the spry inhabitant, old Russ. After the introductions had been made the mail carrier left us to our own devices. I found Russ to be most jovial, possessed of a keen sense of humor and erect of carriage. We had a most delightful three-hour visit.

Astrologically he is a Pisces, born April 7, 1884. The original house erected by Russ's grandfather is long gone. Russ's father and a couple of aunts had been raised in it. Russ has lived in the present house for fifty years, and now it looks it. His wife, who bore them one son is long gone, and the son, now sixty-four, is elsewhere. Of the 350 acres taken up by the grandfather, 130 of them still remain in possession of Russ, and he is in the midst of a hassle with the state over their intent to acquire a goodly portion of the acreage for a freeway passage which Russ claims "isn't necessary; just a political move to spend more money—get some politician's name in the news."

Bright-eyes and clear of speech, thought, and memory, he regaled me with tales of the past: the old mines, the people then living, and the towns that sprang up and disappeared overnight. Sitting there amidst bric-a-brac, some over a century old, and four vintage clocks hanging about on the walls, all keeping time, ticking their metal hearts out, I was delight-

ed I had brought my tape recorder. I recorded the session for
my own interest and shall spend happy hours after he is gone
listening to "what used to be," hearing unpublished stories of
people, places, and things whose memories will otherwise be
interred with him. I've deliberately withheld his last name.
He has surrounded himself with *current* mementos too?
plaques decorate the walls attesting to the gratitude of the
historical society and the museum for the relics and antiques
he has placed in their care for posterity. Now the state is
trying to dispossess him, and the granite-like old-timer isn't
having any of it!

When I told him what I was after—stories of ghosts—his
eyes twinkled, he looked at me for a moment, and then
chuckled.

"There is somebody hanging around here, I got a problem
with them."

"Do you know who they are?"

"Nope. Don't know why they hang around. Guess they
think maybe I'm lonesome and want to keep me company.
Or maybe *they* are lonesome."

"What does he, or it, do?"

"Oh, it moves things around. I put something down, then
when I look for it, it's gone, then I find it, maybe days later,
right where I put it!"

"Russ, I don't mean to be indelicate, and I hope you understand, but could it be that because of your age, perhaps
you forget?"

His answer was immediate and definite.

"Pshaw! I've wondered about that myself. But it isn't so.
It's happened when other people were here, too. Things just
disappeared, and they couldn't find them, either. I've marked
around things with a pencil, put them there on purpose, then

later when I look they are gone, then they are there, right there where I penciled around them."

"Has it happened recently?"

"Sure, it happens all the time. About a month ago a fellow who rents the lower half of my property to grow feed on, came to the house and wrote me a check for the rent. He laid it right there on that table. Then we just sat and talked for some time. Right when he was going to leave, he looked at the table and asked me if I had the check? Well, I hadn't taken it, hadn't even gotten out of this chair, and I told him I didn't have it. The door was open and we figgered the wind had blown it on the floor. He looked all over the table, the floor, then we even went outside to see if it had blown out the door. We couldn't find it. He wanted to write me another check, but I told him to wait awhile, I might find it. Look at that table. There isn't anything on it but that coffee pot, and that's all there was on it the day he wrote the check and laid it there.

"Well, it was three or four days later, and I use that table all the time, when I walked over to it, and laying right there where he put it, was the check. I picked it up and looked at it. It wasn't damp or dirty. Then I heard someone give a loud laugh. They do it all the time. It sounded like it was right here in the room. I looked all around, then opened the door thinking maybe somebody was outside. No one was there. This happens all the time."

"Have they, or it, ever done anything to hurt you?"

"Naw. I get a bit scared sometimes, and wish I had someone here to talk to, but whoever it is here with me doesn't seem mean. I feel them around lots of times, but they don't hurt me, just hide things and make me look for them, then laugh at me. Now I even laugh back at them. If I got mad at them they might get mad at me!"

I was hoping his house guest would manifest somehow while I was there, but it didn't happen, worse luck. I prodded him to remember if anything happened when he was a young man, working the mines, driving stage?

"Well, there was a funny thing happened. It was before my time, in my daddy's time. He told it to me many times, and I heard others talk about it when they would come to the house for dinner or just to chat for a spell.

"There was this fellow, Frank Walker, who drove the stage from Genoa [Nevada] up here. Frank was born and raised in Genoa. It's just down the mountain from Lake Tahoe, on the edge of the Carson Indian Agency. Walker said that he was driving the stage along one afternoon, without any passengers, when all of a sudden he saw a Union soldier standing in the middle of the road. He was dressed in his full uniform, but wasn't carrying any weapon that Frank could see. He was that close to the tongue of the stage that Frank pulled the horses up real hard to keep from hitting him, but the tongue went right through him. The tongue had that metal prong on it, the end of it. Well, the horses bucked and reared a good bit. Frank stopped the stage and got off and walked all around, trying to find that soldier. He didn't find him, and there wasn't any blood or anything on the tongue to show it had gone through someone. When Frank came into the stage stop, my daddy said they didn't believe the story he told, and said he'd been drinking too much, and told him so.

It wasn't long, about a week, when another miner came into Markleeville [California, elevation 6,500 feet] and told the people at the saloon that he'd seen a Union soldier walking across the road, just out of town. He had hollered at him, but the fellow didn't pay any attention, and he just walked right into a bunch of trees by the creek and disappeared.

"A woman and her son rode into Markleeville sometime

later and said they had seen a Union soldier in uniform walking along on the road, going the same direction they were, and they were going to give him a ride. When they got about thirty feet from him, he turned and looked at them and then just disappeared. He wasn't there, just like that. They stopped and called all around, and then they got scared that they'd seen a ghost and took off for town.

"Guess it was about 1950, when a miner came into Gardnerville, that's in Nevada, and told the fellow working at the truck station that he'd seen a guy all dressed up in a Union army uniform, walking along the road. He just thought the guy was one of those kids dressed up the way they do now. Since he was walking kinda close to the road, the driver honked his horn. The soldier looked, and then the driver said he just disappeared! Just like that. That's the only time I've heard the story of the soldier since I was a boy. I wonder who he is, and what is he hanging around here for?"

That's all old Russ could tell me of ghosts. We did have a lively discussion about our philosophies. It was most interesting to hear this uneducated man tell of his belief in continuing life, that we don't really go anyplace when we die. He thinks we've got too much to learn to go right straight to heaven!

"We've got to take it in stages, like from one grade to the next. Me, scared of dyin'? Nope. I'm getting pretty close to it now, but it doesn't bother me. Just hope I've learned whatever it is I'm supposed to have learned this trip. I'd kinda like to come back someday, after I'm gone, and find out who it is that's around here, the one having fun with me." He chuckled and his eyes sparkled with the anticipation of it.

That was the end of the "ghost" stories, and our session. Russ is one of my Most Unforgettable Characters.

I left old Russ, waving goodbye to him as he stood in the door of his home, drove up on top of 8,500-foot Monitor Pass, stopped the car, got out, and just stood for a moment by myself. The vast panorama was impressive; a light wind was blowing the new snow particles which would soon turn into a heavy downfall or perhaps a howling blizzard that would cover the rugged majesty of this upheaved planetary piece of nature; my mind went back over the people and things I'd seen and heard so far on my ghost story hunt. There in the silence, in the midst of the evidence of tremendous energy of nature, it didn't seem possible that with all the violence, misery, and suffering that plague mankind, a person moving to the next, and hopefully, higher plateau of experience would try to remain earthbound, hold grudges and wreak vengeance, forgetting that during his own earthly life he, too, was trying to find his way, looking for help, not hinderance from unseen things. But, as the Spanish so aptly put it, *Asi es la vida*—that is life.

"What's Going On?"

Since it's neither my premise nor right to prove or disprove the existence or veridicality of any of these phenomenal stories, when the title question is asked me I can only fall back on what I've read, observed, or experienced. People who have turned out to be *physical* mediums have called me in a paroxysm of fear, telling me they are experiencing "things" which are scaring them half to death. They are perhaps the most interesting of the mediums. Manifestations occur to them which they've never had before; they know nothing about the paranormal or supernatural except for ghost stories they heard as kids, thrills they felt running past grave yards at night, and hearing the minister or priest warn of evil spirits, etc.

Mental mediums who are unaware of their gift are another class. They hear voices, receive precognitive or retrocognitive information through clairaudience, clairvoyance, telepathy, or let's call it extra sensory perception. There is always the possibility of fraud. Some people, few perhaps, wanting to be known as possessing psychic or mediumistic abilities will go to any lengths to concoct whole series of events which they have woven from a whole shroud; and they are at times difficult to uncover evidentially.

The reason I preface the following story in this manner is to insure against being taken falsely within context or being misconstrued out of context. The young lady I interviewed possesses both physical and mental paranormal abilities. She genuinely desires to find out "what's going on?" The best I could think of was to start at the beginning and have her bring me up to date.

Mrs. Beverly Rostoker was born June 14, 1935, at about 3 P.M., in Denver, Colorado (for the astrology buff), and experienced her first phenomenon when she was about six years old. She has always dreamed in color. Her first memorable dream had to do with a couple of goldfish she had as a child. Either during the night or just prior to awakening in the morning, Beverly had a dream in which she saw one of her two goldfish jump out of its bowl and her grandfather's foot descend on it, killing it. When she awakened, she was so frightened she asked her girlfriend, Gloria, to go in the kitchen and see if her goldfish was really dead. It was. It had happened exactly as she'd dreamed it. Grandpa Sam hadn't meant to step on the fish; it was an accident. She'd had either a precognitive dream, or it was telephathic at the moment of occurrence. At the time she didn't realize or know that her dream was anything paranormal.

The family moved to Los Angeles shortly after that. From time to time Beverly would have what is defined in parapsychology as *deja vu* (the feeling that you have been somewhere or done something before). Her feeling was that she'd been in an earthquake, or earthquakes, at some time; they weren't new to her, and she was scared.

At age sixteen, about eighteen years ago, she became very disturbed and wanted to return at once to Denver. Her parents couldn't dissuade her; she raised the money, and did go back. Her feeling was that California was going to experience a tremendous earthquake and she must run. The day after she left, the huge earthquake occurred as she'd "seen" it, in the Bakersfield-Tehachapi area, northwest of Los Angeles.

Personally sometimes, when I allow it, I feel downright frustrated at not possessing more psychic ability. Yet, from what I've witnessed, many psychics and mediums can become very disturbed people, their gift pulling and hauling them about, making their lives quite uncomfortable, sometimes unbearably so. Again, I add, this does not apply to Mrs. Rostoker; she seems to be quite well balanced, and would just like to find out about herself and the strange things which happen to and around her.

At age twenty, Beverly married, and says she saw almost immediately, clairvoyantly, the birth of the children she was to have and of her divorce. One day her husband came to pick her up after a shopping tour. On the drive home she "knew" a neighbor had just died, and she knew which neighbor it was. She told her husband the name. When they arrived home, almost at once the phone rang and another neighbor told her the person she'd "seen" dead had just passed on. (It must be a gas for a nonbeliever to be married to a psychic!)

About five years ago she had to enter the hospital for about a week for different types of tests. Someone had given her a book on palmistry, and she started reading it. Her grandmother had taught her to read cards, which art the grandmother had learned as a child from a gypsy woman. It wasn't but a couple of days before the interns, doctors, nurses, and patients were coming to her room for palm readings! What actually happened was, Beverly was picking up the people psychically, which had nothing to do with reading the lines on their hands and about which she knew practically nothing. She also found that in talking to people she could go back to their childhood and pick up things which were known only to the person, some information which had been consciously forgotten by the individual.

Recently she met a young man of about twenty-two, and during a conversation she told him that when he was a child he had seen someone drown. The drowning had not occurred in a swimming pool, but in a lake. She described the whole incident, and the boy and his brother were absolutely amazed at the accuracy. Another time, in talking with a girl, Beverly described a complete scene in which the girl had been raped. The girl was horrified because, as she said, no one had ever known about it, she'd never told a soul. It had happened when the girl was very young.

Beverly never knows when the "gift" will manifest. She can be in some public place, like a restaurant, and by looking at some person their complete life will be outlined to her—in color, yet. Many times she follows the strong compulsion to approach the person and speak to them of what she sees. She told one stranger, a man, that he owned a blue Thunderbird, that he was thinking about going through a divorce right now, and that he had two children, a boy and a girl. The man thus faced by a person he'd never seen, telling him intimate details of his life, became angry and wanted to know how the hell she knew him so well and who she was. When she explained that she "saw" those things around him, he told her to get away, far away!

At this point in our interview, I suggested that it might prove beneficial for her to visit a certain astrologer. Perhaps she could find out what made her tick by looking at her horoscope. My own feeling is that there is an answer to most everything; it's merely a matter of finding the right avenue and learning the answer. Isn't that what science does? Astrology is still called a pseudo-science. To indulge myself with a commercial for a moment, I recommended Beverly contact a member of the American Federation of Astrologers, Mrs. Franka Moore, who lives in Canoga Park, California, and lists among her clients many of the top show business (and business and scientific) names. These clients return year after year for a reading of their progressed chart for the following year. Mrs. Moore has been at it for about twenty years, and I've found her to be an honest, most knowledgeable person, with excellent perspicacity. And that's a favorable mouthful considering some so-called astrologists I've visited, with extreme disgust, around the country! Mrs. Moore delineates the natal chart and the progressions, and gives the trends; but she does *not* make predictions.

Now Mrs. Rostoker and I got into the present, and explored what is going on in her West Hollywood home that could be attributable to a poltergeist. The scientific definition of poltergeist is "recurring spontaneous psychokinesis" (RSPK), or "paranormal physical disturbances," i.e. prankish manifestations. The poltergeist is described as a "material object without a physical occupant." It can be unseen, or seen, and usually the experient wants to know, "what's going on?"

Is there some emanation from Beverly Rostoker which causes the phenomena in the house? Is it because she is psychic and can be used as a medium for discarnate spirits to manifest through? Anyway, Beverly had put up a curtain rod, across the top of the doorway between the front room and the bedroom. The rod was hollow, and she hung long strands of beads from it, twelve strands in all, six on each side, leaving the middle portion clear. The strands reached almost to the floor.

The only way to properly itemize the occurrences is by number:

1. At times the whole twelve strands would wave and jump about as though manipulated by someone. (No one was touching them, nothing else in the room was moving.)

2. Sometimes only one strand, or two, one on each end of the twelve strands, would jump and/or sway, violently.

3. The bottom six inches of two or three strands have been observed being swayed back and forth—not the upper portion—as though someone had taken the lower portion in his hand and moved only the portion below the hand.

4. One strand was forcibly pulled off the rod and tossed out onto the middle of the floor, in full view of three witnesses.

5. One night the whole rod was pulled off the door and tossed out onto the front room floor. (After that last one, Beverly didn't put it back up!)

Prior to talking with Mrs. Rostoker, I'd heard about a spoon jumping out of a bowl her young son, Gregory, ten-and-a-half, was eating from. Turning to Gregory I asked him what had happened?

"Well, I was in the kitchen and I was fixing me some chocolate milk in my Flintstone glass (a giveaway from the "Flintstone" TV series), and I was stirring it. I left the spoon in the glass and washed my hands, and when I turned around, I saw the spoon pop out of the glass and land on the sink."

"What did you say, Greg?"

"Well, I called my mother. I said, 'Mother, my spoon popped out of the glass.' She came in and we both looked at it. I put it back in the glass like it had been, but it didn't happen again."

"How did you feel about it, Greg, when it popped out?"

"I thought it was ghosts. We have them in here."

"Do you mind there being ghosts around?"

"Yeah, I don't like it, but they don't hurt us."

Then there was another incident, when Greg was eating his morning cereal. His mother and a friend were sitting across the table from him, also eating. Greg had just taken a mouthful of cereal, returned the spoon to his bowl, sat back and was chewing, when whammo, the spoon jumped, unaided, out of the bowl, and clattered on the table. The other two saw it. (No, the spoon wasn't spring loaded from the "Batman" TV show!)

And how about the day Beverly's father died? The bedroom had been nice and neat when they left to go to her parent's house. When they came back, the room was a shambles. There were books all over the floor. She also has a wooden carved owl, and the owl was kept on top of the dresser. It was thrown on the floor and a big chip broken out of it, and there were chips out of a lot of her bedroom bric-a-brac, from being thrown around. There was no evidence of breaking and entering, nor any robbery. Only Beverly and Greg had keys to the house.

Having occurred within a twelve-hour period of her father's death, this could be classed as a crisis manifestation, i.e., the recently released spirit was making its presence known, especially to those who had been close to it in life. Possibly, if they had been home at the time it arrived, there would have been a visible apparition (crisis apparition).

Another evening, Beverly, a friend named Betty, and Greg were in the bedroom. There is a heavy conical glass paperweight in the article aperture of the headboard. No one was near it, they were not sitting on the bed. Suddenly it took a flying leap from where it was and landed in the middle of the bed. That happened in either September or October of 1969. The girl, Betty, split for the front room, and doesn't like to go into the bedroom! As if that would make much difference to a ghost? Especially if you can't see it!

I noticed a great many very old items, like tapestries, vases, a mirror, some china, placed about or hanging from the walls. I asked if she knew whether any of the people who'd owned the objects were deceased. Two people were who'd given her some of the articles—her grandfather and her father. Whether it is either of them isn't known because they've not materialized or communicated with her, which isn't to say they can't or won't someday, when the conditions are right.

Beverly has felt many times that someone was near her, very close, almost touching her. Other times she's had people in the front room and there have been tappings and rappings on the wall, particularly one wall, which those present have tried to duplicate without success. The raps came not from within the wall, but from the *room* side. They've placed their hands on the wall and felt the vibrations.

A short time ago Beverly was going with a man named Harvey. She kept a planter on top of the refrigerator, and Harvey would remark, because she wouldn't take it down, "I wish that damn thing would break, or you would get rid of it, or I'm going to throw it away." Within a few days after the last request, or threat, they entertained some guests. A couple of the women were in the kitchen keeping Beverly company while she prepared dinner. All of a sudden there was a crash. The two women were sitting at a table, not even near the refrigerator, and they swore they saw the planter take a flying leap into the air and come down with a crash on the floor. It wasn't on the edge of the refrigerator, it was placed well in the middle of it. It would appear the ghost didn't like the damn thing, either!

Beverly has at times become quite annoyed with the ghost and has sincerely and with some asperity tried to talk it into leaving, just go away, or go someplace else. They've had it. It's tiring to never know when something will happen. The last manifestation was less than a month ago, so it's still there at the same old stand, paying no attention to its earthly counterpart's blandishments to leave. Ghosts seem to know who has the proper vehicle of vitality through which they can gain the energy to manifest, so I guess Beverly and Greg are stuck with their phenomenal visitor.

Beverly has already been in contact with Dr. Freda Morris, Ph.D., medical psychologist, Neuropsychiatric Institute, UCLA, who has been investigating the paranormal, supernormal, and supernatural for many years. Yes, the ghost is there.

My last suggestion to Beverly was to have a sitting with a good, developed psychic who might bring through the discarnate who is incumbent in the Rostoker home, find out who he is, and perhaps get on better terms with him. Maybe they need help, it's possible, and they don't know what to do to get attention except by tossing the curtains, flipping spoons, throwing paperweights, hurling planters off refrigerators. To think that a ghost is "after" you just because it does those things isn't fair! Ask any ghost.

What
Do You Think?

Here's the story of a family "lucky" enough to have *two* ghosts. A man and wife previously owned the house in which the present occupants now live. The former shall remain anonymous; the present, six-year tenants are Fred and Sharon Maguire and their two children, Daniel, seven, Davy, four, on Hatteras Street, Tarzana, California. The former owners were both suicides, in the house, at separate times. One was an alcoholic; the other, the wife's downfall, was pills.

Dr. Freda Morris, Ph.D., also put me in touch with this couple for their strange ghostly phenomena. Dr. Morris knows something is going on in the house, and has spent considerable time researching the incidents. Only more time will perhaps bring to light who or what is causing the phenomena plaguing the Maguires. Both Fred and Sharon wish it could be now, get it over with, come to grips (who wants to grip a ghost?) with whatever it is.

There is no easy answer to poltergeist phenomena. Just about the time the experts decide they've pretty well tracked down the physical, motivating agent, the whole *thing* goes up in *smoke*; the theory still only holds about half the water.

The following story doesn't concern the penetration of matter through matter, but it does deal briefly with either observed teleportation, or levitation. The answer could depend on what or who is doing the moving, transporting the objects.

Fred was born December 23, 1937, in New York City, between 1:05 and 1:15 P.M. Sharon was born September 21, 1942, East Los Angeles, at about 3 P.M., give or take a few minutes either way.

The first phenomenon Fred experienced was shortly after they moved into the house. He was in the back storeroom one day, the place where most of the phenomena seem to occur or emanate from. He was running the vacuum cleaner, and over the sound of the cleaner he thought he heard what sounded like a child crying.

There is a small room off the back end of the storeroom which was used by the former owners as a darkroom to develop pictures. Fred turned the cleaner off and he still heard the crying, sobbing, like a small frightened child. The darkroom was closed off by a door. Fred called out to their then only boy, Daniel, but received no answer. He walked to the door of the darkroom and as he reached for the knob, the crying stopped. He went on into the darkroom, turned on the light and looked around. There was nothing there, so he ran back into the house and called for Sharon who said he was "white as a sheet."

It was Fred's first encounter with anything spooky and it does shake you up. They checked the bedroom, where Daniel was sleeping, and all was well. The two kind of forgot about this incident, laying it to "something" outside the house, a noise being bounced off the room from somewhere in the neighborhood. They didn't *want* to believe it was something supernatural!

Some eight months later, they heard what sounded like heavy footsteps in the attic. A human being sounds like a two-footed animal when it walks, not like a cat, or a horse, or a dog. The ceiling and the beams creaked beneath the weight of whatever it was walking up there. They walked from room to room, following underneath the footsteps, and then back again. There was an open window in the attic, so the next day Fred screened it up and the walking stopped, momentarily. The only assumption they could arrive at was that it *was* an animal with two feet; but what kind of a two-footed animal?

Sharon was the next to first hear the footsteps in the attic, when they resumed at another time. She called to Fred and they both stood and listened. Sure enough, the step was heavy, one foot stepping after the other. Then it stopped.

When Peter Hurkos, the renowned psychometrist, was called into the phenomenon, he said that a man had committed suicide in the house, in the darkroom, that the man was an alcoholic. Later, a trance-medium was called in, and in trance she described a woman, the wife, who was on pills, and who had also committed suicide in the house. The trance-medium said that it was the spirit of the woman, not the man, who was remaining with the house.

The spirit plays tricks on Fred, but somehow, for some reason, takes it easy with Sharon, perhaps because, as Sharon says, it would scare her to death if the things happened to her that happen to Fred. Little games, like letting the dog out of the storeroom through either a closed window or a locked door or opening the lock on the door and letting the animal out when Fred has the only key to the lock in his pocket. That has happened many times.

Also in the storeroom is the switch to a spotlight which is

outside the room, and it's been turned on many times when only the dog is in the storeroom. Unless that dog is a lot smarter and more adept with his paws than most dogs, it isn't going to rise on its back feet and snap the switch on with its nose or mouth. Fred raised the dog on its hind legs to its full extended length and it couldn't get high enough to reach the switch.

One rather windy night a few years ago, they stepped outside the front door, closing it, but carefully seeing to it the door wasn't locked. After admiring the night for about fifteen minutes, they attempted to reenter the house, and the door was locked. Luckily, Fred had the key with him. As Sharon says, "It knew we had a key, so it played a trick on us."

Fred plugged in the coffeepot one morning and went into the bathroom. A few minutes later he returned, and the coffeepot was unplugged. No one else was up at the time. If it happened only once it might have been suspect, but the coffeepot incident got to be an irregular occurrence. He would plug it in, it would be unplugged. He would unplug it, it would be plugged in.

They paused here to tell me that there hadn't been any manifestations for about a week, but they have found that when they talk about the "ghost," that seems to reactivate it, and probably now it would begin doing things again. Talking about it gives it the idea perhaps it's been neglecting them!

One Friday, Sharon made coffee. She plugged the pot onto the cord and then went about her business. Shortly, Fred came in and checked to see if the coffee was ready. Finding the pot not only unplugged, but the cord gone as well, he asked Sharon where it was. She was as mystified as Fred. The cord had been plugged into both the pot and the electric outlet, and now was completely missing. The cord was missing for three days, and then, after having used her laundry basket practically daily, as a mother will who has to service two young children and two adults, she found the cord neatly coiled up, in the bottom of the empty laundry basket.

Whoever or whatever is present seems to do Sharon's bidding at times. The Englebert Humperdink record had been played and played in the house, for the kids, for neighbors, for whomever showed up, and Sharon finally made the remark she was getting pretty tired listening to it. The next day the album was gone. It was missing for two weeks. Sharon cleaned the house most every day, dusting everywhere about the rooms, high and low. The kids had plagued both parents for the record, and Sharon finally addressed the "spirit," imploring it to bring back the album, if it had, indeed, taken it. That night while she was watching TV with Fred, she had a strong urge to go into the bedroom. There, on the dresser lay the album. She accused Fred of putting it there, but he was as puzzled over its reappearance as she was.

Again, Peter Hurkos, after paying them another visit, predicted there would be some activity with pots and pans within two weeks. At about the end of the two-week period, Dr. Freda Morris came over to the house and stayed two nights, waiting for some manifestation. Dr. Morris missed the pots and pans incident, but it did happen, a few nights later.

The Maguires have a large collie dog, and an assortment of stray and neighbor animals come over to take pot luck with them almost every evening. There was a small bucketful of water, and about five pans of varying sizes sitting around the back door. All the utensils disappeared, the bucketful of water, and the feeding pans. They looked high and low; not a trace could be found. Fred searched the whole area, including inside the house, went into other people's back yards to try and find them. Where are you going to hide a three-gallon pail, as Fred asked? He even went up into the attic to see if their ghost had spirited them up there. Nothing. That was on a Wednesday. They found the utensils, all of them the following Saturday. Fred had gone into the storeroom where they kept Laddie, the collie, to let him out for the day, and he almost stepped into the water bucket. All the utensils were there, piled neatly right inside the door. The water in the bucket had begun to turn green as water will do when left standing, especially in warm weather. Wherever it had been it hadn't been disturbed, and was getting stale. Fred and Sharon then remembered, between them, that Peter Hurkos had said it would happen around the middle of the week, like a Wednesday. Anyway, the reporters got hold of the story, and there was a flurry of press excitement over where the pots and pans had been for three days and bearing particular attention upon Peter Hurkos's prediction of the time of the occurrence.

Sharon was feeding her youngest son one day, and also had the TV on. She had prepared some food, gotten a bottle of vitamins out of the cupboard, and taken a tablet from the bottle. As she dropped the tablet into a glass which was going to have orange juice added to it, she flicked her eyes briefly to the TV set. When she looked back at the glass, the tablet wasn't in the glass. Of course she couldn't tell if it had dropped back into the bottle which she still held in her other hand, but that was questionable. Something caught her eye off to one side of the glass, which was sitting on the sink. The tablet was in mid air, just hanging there (if a pill can hang). There was no shelf, nothing under it or holding it. What had levitated it or teleported it? Or should I say, who? As she watched, transfixed, or horrified, or both, the tablet slowly settled down to the sink top. It didn't fall down, it gently came down to rest. Complete defiance of all the known laws of gravity.

The case of the kids' train is a real grabber. As you read this next incident, put yourself in the Maguires' place, try to figure what you would do, what you would think, how you would feel.

The kids had been given an electric train for Christmas. It had all the usual accoutrements—whistles, bells, motor sounds—the whole gamut. The train was in the kids' room. Sometime in the middle of the night it turned on, everything worked; then there was a crash. In the deep silence of night, a phenomenon like that is quite loud! Sharon was the first to gain wakefulness, quick like, and she was up and dashing for the bedroom even before the crash. She dashed quickly into the bedroom, next to the master bedroom, where the children were sleeping. Turning on the light she immediately observed that both boys had been asleep, but were now stirring—and who wouldn't with all the racket. The train had been placed on top of the dresser at the time the kids went to bed, and now it was lying on the floor, upside down, wheels spinning, bells clanging, whiste tooting, etc. Sharon reached down, turned it over and snapped the switch off. The kids were awake now, and she wanted to know which one had knocked the train off the dresser? Neither of them had been out of bed, and Daniel, to whom the train belonged, wanted to know if it was broken.

Fred is an electronics engineer, and the next day he took the machine completely apart, and there was no way in which he could make it turn on except by snapping on the switch. He crossed wires, tried to short the circuit out. No way. He put an ohmmeter on it, then a volt-ammeter. Nothing was wrong with the electrical system. It *had* to be snapped on.

At the end of last summer, Fred was taking down the outside window cooler to store it—the one that serviced the front room. The boys were both out in the front yard with him. Fred picks up the incident here.

"I visibly saw the window shade being pulled aside, and what sounded like a child's voice, or someone imitating it, said, 'Peek-a-boo.' I figured someone was playing games with me, so I went inside to see who it was. No one was in the room, and I looked all around in it. Sharon was outside, in the back. I saw the shade move, as if somebody had gripped the shade from behind, where you couldn't see the hand, and I saw the shade wrinkle just as it would do if you take hold of it, and then moved it aside. It was getting dark, and it was dark in the room, so all I could see was blackness when the shade was pulled aside. I might add that I've never seen any physical body."

At this point Sharon broke in and strongly emphasized that she didn't *want* to see anyone. She preferred that her "friend" remain invisible, if she had to be there at all. I'm inclined to be on her side, but at the same time, knowing there is someone in the house with you, it would bug me if I didn't know what they looked like!

They've both had the feeling they've seen "something" out of the corner of their eyes, caught a fleeting glimpse, but when they turned toward it, nothing was there. Just the feeling of a presence. Sharon did awaken one night, and in turning over, looked toward the door. She saw what she thought was a female figure standing in the doorway, outlined by the light of the moon coming in the window. She watched for a moment, and then it was gone. She would rather attribute it to moon shadows than to think their guest is beginning to get up enough power to materialize. The "woman" had short hair, was fairly tall, or was standing off the floor, floating. She couldn't tell how it was dressed, if it was dressed. Since then she's not left the door even only halfway open—she's shut it!

When you get involved with ghosts, or suspected ghosts, and you talk openly about it, the word gets out a lot farther than you think. You never know who is going to show up next with either a theory, a method of exorcising them, or an offer to make direct contact with the discarnate/excarnate. Sometimes the results are gratifying, satisfying, or they can be hilarious or traumatic.

A young woman showed up who said she used a dowsing method to get answers from spirits, and would like to try it for them. She uses a couple of coat hangers, bent especially for her purpose, and suggested they use coat hangers from the Maguire house, as the spirit would feel more familiar. The hangers were produced and suitably bent into rods, the hand end being about five inches in length, then bent at a ninety degree angle to form the long ends which were the sensors.

The rods open for a Yes answer, close for a No answer. To help preclude your hands operating independently of each other, you grasp the rods, then place your thumbs together (so the positive hand won't attract or influence the negative hand). The first question asked was, "Is there a spirit present in the house?" The rods opened for the answer Yes.

Fred held the rods, and when a Yes or No question was asked, he could feel the rods turning. He squeezed them as tightly as he could to keep them from turning, and still they turned. Try the rods yourself and you will note (maybe) that if you don't touch your thumbs together as you bring your hands to within about four inches of each other, the tips of the rods will be attracted to each other as if magnetized. When I tried it, touching thumbs, the tips generally went apart, and I apparently received a Yes answer for a question I'd not asked! This isn't to say the method doesn't work, but it's so restricted in its use that perhaps I was skeptical. I halfway expected the rods to swing clear around and bang me on the shoulders for playing around with them (it).

Both the Maguires had had the current flu bug which plagued the San Fernando Valley during the winter, and had prescriptions from the doctors, which they kept in the medicine cabinet in the bathroom. The pills disappeared. When the dowser-type woman asked if the spirit had taken them, the rods opened up and answered Yes. They walked from room to room asking if the pills were present in that room. No. When they got to the den and asked the question, the rods opened up to Yes. They went to each side of the room and asked the question, "Are the pills on this side of the room?" When they got to the closet and asked if the pills were in there they got a Yes. Fred and Sharon said they felt like fools, but willing to go along with the woman, they began exploring the closet, taking everything out and searching the clothing. Way in the back of the closet, in a cubicle containing clean towels, were the bottles. They were the bottles which had their names on them, typed by the druggist. That would figure! It was the woman who'd committed suicide. She was a pill-head, and like the alcoholic, they hide their supply so they'll always have some on hand.

It has been impossible for the Maguires to keep pills in the house. Fred had some amphetamines and some sleeping pills, and they kept disappearing. He had put them up high in the back storeroom to keep them away from the children. They disappeared and have never been found. The bottle containing Fred's prescription for the amphetamines had been used up with the exception of one tablet.

One night he laid out that last pill, to take when he awakened in the morning. When he reached for it next morning, no pill. There are certain effects produced by the ingestion of this certain type medication, and neither Sharon nor the kids exhibited them. There would have been a definite recognizable reaction. Where was the pill? Two days later Fred put on a pair of pants he hadn't worn for about a week. When he reached into the back pocket, there was the pill. What was identifiable—the pill he'd laid out was broken in two and so was the one he found in the trouser pocket. Coincidence?

As in the case of "Old Russ," "something" moved his things around, snitched papers and objects, then returned them when it suited the spirit. Cases of people being bombarded by stones, bricks, nails, pieces of coal, most all of them falling or being thrown from "thin air," are not by any means unknown, and have been reported throughout history. Sometimes one of the recipients of this teleportive deluge has been injured, but not often.

When matter penetrates matter you have something else to contend with. How can matter penetrate matter, and retain its original shape? The object thusly teleported, when handled immediately after its appearance, has been reported to have been warm.

Carl Gustav Jung, famous Swiss psychologist, and an excellent parapsychologist, stated that in his investigations of teleportation, there was usually an adolescent living in the house, or at least present on the premises, and they were the focus of the poltergeist phenomena which was brought about, said Jung, by their inner tensions, frustrations, aggressive behavior, and repressed rage. Somehow human psyche and matter are entangled, so that powerful psychological states and external events can be triggered by extreme emotional and psychic energies. These at times result in what is known as poltergeist phenomena (mischievous ghost). This is, of course, still theory, but scientists and investigators have to move slowly, checking everything two and three times over, noting every *possible* possibility. No doubt one day the answer, or perhaps a partial answer, will be forthcoming, but until then the bulk of the world's people believe in ghosts—departed spirits remaining after physical death, and some of them most active! What do you think?

Indian Ghosts

Just a Bunch
of Kids

A tortured manifestation of nature called Little Lake, California, lies athwart State Routes 6 and 395, 168 miles northwest of Los Angeles. It would be difficult for a motorist to miss Little Lake unless he was driving through in the black of night. Thousands of years ago, three adjacent volcanoes erupted simultaneously and lent their combined westward lava flow to form a massive black cliff that terminates abruptly at Little Lake. The lake is in a natural depression at the foot of one portion of the four-mile-long cliff.

In 1948 my wife and I stopped at Little Lake to watch a group of archeologists digging at the base of the cliff. A Dr. Harrington, head of the expedition, told us they had unearthed proof that eight to fifteen thousand years ago a race of Indians had lived at the spot where they were digging. He showed us some pottery, bones, and charcoal, and some obsidian arrowheads, all of which they'd dug up at a depth of thirty feet. He also exhibited large pieces of petrified palm root. The area had been subtropical when the Indians lived there. The Indians had scouted thirty miles over the lava flows to find the black glassy obsidian. Dr. Harrington also pointed out above us the place where a waterfall had carved its niche in the hard lava.

This group of Indians who had lived eight to fifteen thousand years ago had buried their dead in a sitting position in vases of oil, and a few of these had been found in the area. This had been Indian country long, long before the white man arrived. Would it be strange then, their subconscious minds containing all memory, for some of the Indians to return for a visit to the scene of their earthly life?

A very short distance from Little Lake lives a hardy soul named Edith. She and her husband moved to the present abode twelve years ago. Edith's husband passed on, as the saying goes, about five years ago, and she remained there, alone in the house he'd built. She supports herself by leasing land which contains a pumice deposit her husband had discovered.

One night, two years ago, Edith was rudely awakened by a loud crashing and banging in the kitchen of her four-room home. She had no animals, and could only think the house was being ransacked by thieves or vandals. She sat up, trying to collect her awakening thoughts. It sounded as if all the pots and pans in the kitchen were being kicked and thrown around. Edith is no cowering female. She grabbed the .38 revolver she kept on the night table, turned on the bedside light, got up, threw a gown about her, and headed for the kitchen fully expecting to find at least a number of miscreants, maybe drunks, who'd broken in. When she snapped on the kitchen light she at least expected to see *some*one. The room was a shambles, metalware strewn all over the place. She immediately went to the only outside door in the room, tried it. It was locked, as were the two windows. There wasn't a soul present. Earthquakes are by no means unknown in that area of the San Andreas Fault and the only possible conclusion she could draw was the house had been rocked by a trembler. Something was wrong with that, too. She checked the rest of the house and no other room had been disturbed. Earthquakes are strange bedfellows, but they've never been known to quake only one room of a four-room house! She replaced all the utensils and went back to bed and nothing more happened that night. The following morning she drove to Little Lake post office to see if she had any mail and also to make some inquiries.

"Was there an earthquake last night?"

"Nope, didn't feel none. Didn't hear anything on the radio about one."

She returned to the house, more puzzled than scared, but quite positive she'd picked up kitchen utensils that had been thrown around by something or "someone."

For the next two nights the same thing happened. She would get into bed around 10:30 P.M., and around 11 P.M. the gosh-awful clatter and bang would take place in the kitchen. Only the utensils were scattered about the room. By the third night her nerves were getting pretty well strung out. She got into bed but didn't even try to sleep ... just lay there, waiting. At the appointed hour the clatter began, but this time it was more of a clumping and thumping as if solid dull objects were being thrown around the floor. She got up, grabbed the gun, and ran into the kitchen. Edith's husband had built a shoe rack in one corner of the room, and it was usually full of varied footwear as she had left his shoes in the rack after his death. All the shoes were strewn about the room! Only the shoes, and one piece of kitchenware—a cookie jar! It was lying on its side, the contents spilled out on the sink counter.

How long can this sort of eerie thing go on before the most well-balanced person will begin to suspect something mighty unnatural is taking place? You come to feel you are either losing your mind or being haunted. Edith was pretty well convinced she was being haunted. She'd thrown out the earthquake idea, so there had to be some other answer. True, whatever it was had only bothered inanimate objects, but how long would it be before "it" or "they" took a notion to toss her about, or worse?

In Beatty, Nevada, there is a woman who does card reading, is reputed to be a good psychic. She did a reading for me not long ago, and I can report that two of the many things she told me have come true. Beatty is 104 miles due east of Lone Pine, California, and 134 miles from Edith's house. She made the trip in about an hour and a half, the roads being that lightly traveled when the temperatures in Death Valley are over 120 degrees. It was the morning of the fifth day after the beginning of the strange occurrences.

For those who've not experienced a card reading, the reader has the sitter shuffle the cards a couple of times, then cut them. The personal contact with the pasteboards by the sitter is supposed to transmit emanations to them, arrange them perhaps, maybe place them in some order so that when they are manipulated, thrown down by the reader, she (or he) can pick up on questions or answers. For the card readers who are psychic it is pure and simple (simple if you can do it) psychometry. It has been my own experience that actually the cards have nothing to do with what a psychic reader receives because they are concentrating on "listening," "feeling," vocalizing the impressions they get, and sometimes those impressions are allegedly picked up from someone who is working with the sitter or has knowledge of them on the "other side," the spirit world. Edith knew enough not to give any information or reason for her visit, other than just having a sitting.

No names came through as to who was supplying the information, but Edith was told that a bunch of excarnate Indian kids were visiting her house each night, they didn't mean any harm, they were just having fun! Also, she was not to be afraid, and when next the kids arrived, she was to march right in and shoo them off! No word came through concerning the identities of the kids.

On the drive back to her house, Edith stopped in to talk with a couple who live up the road from her. They were so interested in the story and the possibilities they insisted on spending the night in her haunted house. People who have lived up in the desert or mountain areas for any length of time have come to believe more than disbelieve in such tales and carryin's on, and many of them have anecdotes of their own about strange happenings.

There was no pretense of sleep that night by any of them. They sat in the darkened living room, leaving the kitchen door closed, and waited. Around 11 P.M. they heard the thumping and clumping of objects being thrown about. Followed by her two friends, Edith marched right into the kitchen, snapped on the light and with the imperious tones of a mother correcting her mischievous children, demanded they stop all this nonsense and foolishness—"Get out, don't come back. Shoo, shoo, shoo."

Evidently the "kids" took the shooing in the manner which it was intended. Edith's house hasn't been bothered since with visitations from the excarnate Indian kids who were just having a little fun at the expense of solid flesh-and-blood earthlings.

The Indian
Who Forgot His
Blanket

Since we are still in the Little Lake area and talking about visitations or materializations by the Indians who perhaps lived thereabouts, let's recount what happened to Luisa and Jose Armendariz.

The young couple had been married in San Diego, in September 1968. Early in October, Jose got time off from his job to take a belated honeymoon trip with his bride. They headed for the High Sierras, making the drive only as far as the area of Little Lake, and took a motel room for the night. The motel is about five miles north of the lake.

After having dinner in the restaurant, they sat out front in what might be called the yard—no grass, only a few desert cactus and some creosote bushes. In October the days are usually hot, but the nights cool off quite rapidly after dusk, and before morning it is most comfortable to use a blanket. The two turned in about 10:30 P.M. Jose went almost immediately to sleep after the long drive. Luisa stayed awake and read a magazine. As far as Luisa can remember it was perhaps an hour later when she began to get what she describes as "chilly." She pulled the blanket up over both herself and Jose, and continued to read. The chill continued to build up; she became quite cold, and her teeth began to chatter. Then she felt someone else was in the room.

Not moving from the position in which she was lying facing the door, she glanced up and saw a figure standing in the open doorway, which had been left open as the outside porch was screened. The figure, according to Luisa, was sort of transparent. She thought she could see through it. The equally startling aspect of the apparition was that it was definitely a male, an Indian, and he was absolutely nude!

The only item the figure was wearing that could be called an article of clothing was a twisted thong about his head. There was seemingly no threat from the intruder. He was smiling—just standing there smiling. Luisa was scared and cold. In fact, she was shaking uncontrollably. A few rough jabs in the ribs awakened Jose, and he sat up, asking what the matter was. Luisa pointed toward the door, and Jose saw the same figure, sans clothing, smiling.

Although Jose may have been superstitious, he didn't at that moment "see" through their intruder. There was a naked male in his room and he was understandably outraged, possessed of the natural instinct to protect his mate. He jumped out of bed, reached down and picked up one of his shoes on the way. In one long step he reached the middle of the room, reared back and heaved the shoe. It sailed with unerring aim, but instead of colliding with the visitor and knocking him flat, it went right through him and hit the screened porch behind him. The figure immediately vanished.

Jose, thinking he'd missed, picked up a chair and approached the door, believing the man had stepped aside to hide. As he reached the door he stepped out quickly and slammed the chair against the wall where he thought the man was hiding.

Luisa had begun to add her yells of terror to the melee and it wasn't but a couple of minutes before the manager and another guest arrived to inquire what the trouble was. All they saw was an enraged nude Jose, with a broken chair back, beating at shadows on the screen porch and adding the proper Spanish epithets to accentuate the blows. Both Jose and Luisa told their story at the same time.

When they'd finished the narrative, the manager sorrowfully asked them not to spread the word around. Yes, for some time his motel had been bothered by the apparition of a naked Indian hanging around. Chairs, bottles, and shoes had been thrown at him, and once he'd been fired at with a pistol. He only appeared at night, and at least one of the people present during an earlier materialization had reported the extreme cold, the chills, and physical shaking Luisa had experienced.

To the skeptics, those who wouldn't believe such manifestations even though fully awake and sober and witnessing the materialization of a long-dead, close relative, I invite you to stop at the motel in the Little Lake area, ask about the Indian who stays with them. Maybe they will tell you about him, perhaps not. If you feel so inclined, stay the night, and if he shows up, the least you can do is toss him a blanket—or a serape. I've been asked not to reveal the name of the motel he's chosen as his teepee. You'll have to find it yourself; I did.

Get
Out of Here

This is another story of a materialization. It was told me by Earl Richardson, Lone Pine, California, October 1969. Upon inquiring around I found Earl to be a moderate, temperate man of solid habits.

In the 1930s Earl had an Indian friend named George. (I've never been able to find out why so many Indians are named George and Jim). George is dead now, of old age. For some reason George wanted Earl to get rich. He wanted nothing for himself, just for Earl to have money. Earl had helped George and his family over some rough spots during the depression and perhaps this prompted the wealth-thought for his white friend.

The Indians didn't pan gold like the white man. They would come in with a handful or bottleful of nuggets, and seldom has it been known for an Indian to divulge where he picked them up. When queried, he will get vague, point and say "out there," with a sweeping gesture, taking in half the horizon. The search for minerals by the whites has cost the Indian his culture, country, and life.

Anyhow, in the 1950s when the tungsten rush began in the Alabama Hills adjacent to Lone Pine, old George began going out to see if he could find a claim to stake for Earl. Tungsten is an elusive mineral to find by day. It can be found by its extreme weight, but blacklamping at night with a fluorescent light is the best method. Earl finally bought a lamp for George, "seein's as how he might just come up with something!"

The temperatures in Lone Pine range from some ninty-five to one hundred degrees in the summer, with high humidity, to way below zero during the winter. It's not always that cold, but in flashes, blizzards hit with tremendous fury.

One evening George had tramped out into the Alabamas for a few hours of prospecting. He'd not found anything, and began retracing his steps, blacklamping as he went. George wasn't young at the time and it had turned pretty cold. He sat down behind a rock for a few minutes to get out of the wind and to rest. Then he went to sleep.

How much later, George didn't remember, but he was awakened by somebody calling his name. He opened his eyes, and there before him stood a friend who had been dead for about ten years. The friend, Jim, was looking mighty serious. He waved his arms excitedly, like he'd done in life when he talked, "George, get up and get out of here."

George was fully awake now, but thought he could be dreaming. Jim was dead. "Jim, what are you doing here? You went away many years ago."

"I know, I know. Don't you remember, this is how I died. I was caught by the cold and the snow. You buried me in the canyon, remember?"

George pulled himself to his feet, still undecided about what was going on, but the Indians are more inured, more accustomed to visits from their dead friends and relatives. George said they just stood there for a few moments, two old friends looking at each other across the invisible gulf that separates us from that which we long for but fear to experience. Finally, Jim became authoritative again. He pointed toward Lone Pine. "Go, now. Do not wait. Get out of here."

With that he disappeared, poof, as George told Earl when relating the story. George didn't wait. He made his way into Lone Pine, and within two hours a blizzard hit the slope and the town that would have downed a strong pack animal. For many years old George told the story—that and other stories of meeting and talking with departed friends and relatives—until his old friend Jim (now called "The Rescue Man") has become a living legend of the Alabama Hills.

Who knows but what old George was a psychic, did see Jim and take his advice, and did see all the friends and relatives he talked about. It does happen you know, quite frequently. To say that all occult or ghostly tales are merely myths, legends, or figments of the imagination would not in any wise be completely true, nor wholly false for that matter. There is some phantasy in any narrative of an incident which is not written down immediately. Take for example an auto accident; two people will report it with some slight difference, depending upon the angle from which each was viewing it, their distance from it, the evocation of memory it elicited within them, the level of education, the facility of reporting, etc. Let some time elapse, query the same witnesses, and the difference will have become even more marked. The nitty-gritty kernel is that the accident did take place. That it is embellished with the passage of time doesn't diminish the fact of the occurrence.

Separating the wheat from the chaff isn't easy, but when you've experienced a number of your own ghosts, interviewed dozens of people who've had ghostly manifestations of their own, you can listen with a less jaundiced ear and see that there is a pattern present in visitations, manifestations, and materializations. My wife doesn't go marketing every day, but when she does go there is the same pattern, the same *modus operandi.* Most of the stories emanating from the Old West, the ghost towns, tales about the old-timers, the incidents of one hundred years ago are usually passed along orally for some time before being written down. The majority of them have been souped up either in the telling or in the writing. The individuals to whom the occult has happened, along with the people who repeat their stories second hand, believe in them, usually swear by them, and therein lies the truth, to them. The stories become part of the local history and lore. To argue with them would defeat my own purpose!

The One-Sided Battle

It is most difficult for me to get away from Lone Pine, California, that fascinating area of fact and fiction, the town that has endured Indian uprisings, earthquakes, and has even endured the depletion of its lake waters to provide water for Los Angeles, that burgeoning octopus to the south. In the early days of Lone Pine the whites had only the earthquakes and the Indians to worry about. Sometime, not too long after the Civil War, a batalion of troops was bivouacked along a creed west of town, near what is now called Portal Road. At that time there was trouble between the whites and the Paiute Indians because the whe whites were taking Indian land, and the Indians were waging a shameful(!) resistance. The battalion was moved in to restore and maintain order. During their stay, there were numerous instances of hit and run raids by the Indians on the troop encampment.

That was over one hundred years ago, and now we focus our time camera on Lone Pine of the 1960s, and introduce a new character, a lady named Alice. Alice had moved to Lone Pine and taken up residence in a house near Portal Road creek. She knew nothing at that time of the troops or Indians who'd previously inhabited the location. One evening just after dusk, Alice was preparing dinner in her kitchen, which overlooked the creek. Suddenly she heard gunshots, lots of them. Peering out of the window she saw an Indian standing with his back to her, dressed in full regalia. He turned and looked at her. He was not an Indian, he was a Negro. He was armed with a rifle but made no move toward her, just looked at her for a moment, then turned his attention to the front, away from her and across the creek. Looking beyond him, Alice saw other Indians crouching behind a fallen tree, firing across the creek at some buildings on the other side. From time to time, some of them would fall back to reload. They would look at her. There were eight of them according to Alice's count. The battle went on for about fifteen minutes. She wasn't as scared as she was fascinated. If any of the gunfire had been returned at the Indians from the attacked position, her house would have been hit. She didn't hear thuds or ricocheting bullets.

Suddenly, as is so common with these replays of the memory camera, it was over. The Indians and the Negro just vanished.

Alice ran down to her neighbor's house, about three hundred yards away, and told them the whole story. They hadn't heard the gunfire, but if she thought she did, they would go see what had happened. After reaching the spot where the attackers had held forth they proceeded across the creek to the old buildings, long abandoned. Though they searched carefully, they could find no evidence of new bullet holes in the wooden structures. They did find old holes which could have been made by bullets!

Yes, they believed her, because they'd heard too many stories like this to be complete disbelievers. Alice told her story to the historian in Lone Pine. The old records did indeed tell of not one but many episodes, or attacks, right there. Negroes were numbered amongst the Indians since they probably received better treatment from the red man than from the white.

The story has become one of the unexplained legends of Lone Pine. Or is it a phantasy. How about the "old holes" that could have been made by bullets?

One afternoon, in full daylight, on the other side of Owens Lake, which is right out of Lone Pine, during the days when a narrow-gauge railroad snaked along the mountainside, four passengers in different parts of the train saw a full-scale battle between troopers and Indians. Troopers and Indians alike were shot from the saddle, as they hit the ground they bounced! Dust rose from the pounding hooves, horses neighed and bucked, there were shouts, hollers, and shots. When the train reached Lone Pine the excited passengers told of the battle. The battle was verified as having actually taken place right there, sixty-four years before!

Guard
the Treasure

Before we leave Lone Pine, one more personal story must be told by Earl Richardson, that gentleman who has contributed much to my ghostly pursuit thereabouts.

Perhaps you know it, perhaps you don't, but Lone Pine is a mecca for hunters and fishermen. Unless they put a top on the number of them, sporting-goods stores and gas stations would outnumber the inhabitants! Movie companies from Hollywood have been using the area for many years as a location for literally hundreds of Westerns, and in more recent years, it's been the background for television series.

In 1870, Indians were more numerous than the invading whites. Relations were reasonably comfortable. One group of Indians lived up on Hog Back Creek, about ten miles from town, and kept pretty much to themselves, that is, barring an occasional sortie against the whites. One day some of the braves had a bright idea. They waylaid a government pack train and ran off with what is reputed to have been well in excess of $10,000 in gold coins sent from Washington, D.C. to pay Army troops and to buy up the script that had been issued for supplies and horses. When the marauding braves returned expecting to be treated like heroes, the head man did a little panic dance at the thought of the whites tracking the gold to their door and had it buried in a deep hole, right on the spot. Indians with that kind of money would be highly suspect, and not only the government, but all the thieves and thugs for miles around would descend on them. One brave was detailed to keep constant watch over the cache. No one was to go near it or even talk about it, on pain of expulsion from the tribe. This tantalizing situation existed for the better part of twenty-five years. The gold became almost a legend among the younger Indians who'd never seen it. Our guard aged into his sixties, but he remained alert; this was his lifelong mission, and he carried out his orders in exemplary style.

Along about then, settlers had moved further out from the center of Lone Pine, and a hose cart to fight fires was thought necessary for the protection of homes being built along the creek. Where did they build the one-room firehouse? Right over the spot where the gold had been buried. How did our zealous guard take it? He got into a beef with one of the homesteaders because he was being denied access to his guard post, and got himself killed. He was buried by his people in their burial ground not far from the firehouse. Allegedly, the head man, now rather elderly, attended the funeral service, and is said to have implored the spirit of the man to return or stay there to guard the hoard of gold planted under the firehouse. Evidently that's what happened; the departed spirit stayed; because the legend of the haunted firehouse grew and remained a healthy story for many years. It wasn't known by the whites why it was haunted; it was just haunted.

By 1946 the legend was all but forgotten except, perhaps, by a few old Indians. This is when Earl Richardson first came onto the scene and took up quarters at the exact spot. In fact, Earl stayed the first night in the old firehouse, such as it was. His family slept in the trailer they'd pulled out to the location with them. Earl had bought the plot of land and was going to build a house. From now on the story becomes Earl's personal recounting.

"That piece of ground where the building was, and where my house is now, was part of what had been called 'The Old Cain Ranch.' It had been auctioned off and I bought that part. We're about three hundred yards off the Portal Road, which leads up to Mount Whitney.

"I'm not sure, but somewhere around one o'clock in the morning, I was awakened by something pushing heavily on my chest. The push, or whatever it was, was vicious, like someone pushing you in anger. At first I sat up, thinking I was having a heart attack, but again the heavy weight, which is the only way I can describe it, pushed on my chest. It pushed me down on the mattress. Boy, that scared me. I laid there, trying to get my breath and collect my senses. I knew I'd been pushed by somebody.

"The moon was shining in the open door, and I could see the trailer parked just outside. I was afraid to move. Then I began to get real cold. Big chills ran all over me, big ones. I thought, 'I must be getting sick.' Then I tried to get up again, and the third time I was pushed down by that weight, pushed back, like someone using both hands. This time I stayed down and just laid there wondering what in the world to do. Chills, chills, chills.

"The Indians I'd met have a musky odor about them, from their bodies and from sitting in hogans or houses right in the smoke from their fires. I began to smell that odor. Then I heard shuffling, as if someone was walking around the small room. My biggest fright was when I began to see the outline of a body. I kept watching it, and it kept getting plainer until I could see it was an Indian. He was dressed in some kind of pants, a leather jacket; his hair was long and tied back of his head. I couldn't see his feet, but as he moved I could hear the shuffling.

"He didn't come near me, again, but kept pacing around, like a caged animal, stopping once in awhile to look at me. He didn't look mean or happy, he just looked. I knew better than to try and get up, I just knew he would push me down. It was probably only a few minutes, but it seemed like hours to me when he finally went to the door, turned and looked at me, then stepped outside and although I could see him, he just disappeared."

Earl told me that his chills stopped almost at once following the disappearance. He got up and looked outside but all was quiet. He didn't say anything to his family, but for the next three days his chest was sore from the pushing he'd received.

"Nothing happened the next night, nor the next, so I just more or less forgot about it, except as I say, my chest was sore. I knew I'd seen what I'd seen, and the Indian had done what he did, pushed me down."

The Richardsons went ahead and built the house, and lived in it for fifteen years. "My bedroom was upstairs, right over the spot where the old building housing the fire cart had been. I slept in that bedroom and my wife and the kids slept in the one next to it, on the same floor. One night when my wife and the kids were visiting in Los Angeles, I was awakened by I don't know what. I laid there, fully awake, and all of a sudden I began to have tremendous chills, going up and down me, from the top of my head to my feet. I was really shaking. I though, 'My gosh, what am I getting? I've got something. Shall I get out of bed and go downtown and stay in a friend's apartment, so I can get something to take care of me.' I didn't feel sick, but those chills went on."

Some years had passed since Earl's first encounter with the "presence" of the Indian, and special issue should be made about the chills, the same chills he'd had when the Indian materialized in 1946. "I felt a presence, just like the one I had the first time. I definitely felt someone lean over me, close enough to hear breathing. The chills became larger, I shook so much the bed rattled. I didn't sleep anymore."

He didn't get out of bed, feeling it was safer to stay right where he was. He turned his back to the room and tried to blot out whatever or whoever it was in there with him. "Boy, was I glad when dawn came, and the sun came up!"

It is an established fact from records of this sort of manifestation, from all over the globe, that in order for a departed spirit to materialize it is necessary for them to draw on what we have already referred to as the *vehicle of vitality* of the physical body of a living mortal. This drawing on the vitality is what causes the tremendous chills which in almost every case accompany a materialization, otherwise it seems the spirit could be felt, but not seen.

"For many years after moving into the house I have felt a presence, but it didn't cause me the chills. I have talked with my neighbor who lives about two hundred yards down the creek from me and he has reported, without me telling him, that he has felt a presence in his house. Sometimes, and this is strange, when I get into the bathtub at night, suddenly there is a loud banging like a window being pulled down hard, a door being swung shut, clumps and thumps coming from my bedroom.

"A couple of times I've gotten my gun and gone looking to see if someone is trying to get in. I've never found anyone.

I checked my water heater, it's on the other side of the house and the pipes don't go through my bedroom. I've tried to talk to the Indians around here about it but they just clam up and can't, or won't tell me anything, act like they don't know what I'm talking about, but I can tell by their eyes they know something. I've thought of digging under the house to see if I can find the gold, but just haven't done it. My wife is afraid something really bad might happen to me."

"Earl, when was the last time you had anything happen to you?"

"Within the last year. I've felt the presence at the head of the stairs, usually. I have little chills, but haven't seen him again. Maybe I've gotten used to the chills and feeling his presence; it doesn't scare me as much as it used to. If I ever get those BIG chills again I know I will see him."

Let's Call Him Charley

He was an Indian. He lived near what is now a dry-lake bed in Panamint Valley, just over the hill from Death Valley. It is fifty miles east of Lone Pine, California, and fifty-four miles from a desolate spot which was to become famous as Death Valley Scotty's Castle, on the rim of Death Valley. Charley and another brave had been raised in the same tribe, had hunted together many times, shared good and bad times along with the others, but when the two fell in love with a local maiden, they became bounden enemies. It looked as though Charley was going to win the suitor contest, but his rival did him in by stabbing him with a knife, killing Charley physically dead. Now that should be the end of the story, except to add that the survivor won the hand of the dusky maiden. But the excarnate Charley had other ideas and the story continues.

It has long been known among the Indians that if a warrior is killed while engaged in accomplishing a mission, he, as an excarnate, will continue to work at it. In this case, the medicine man, knowing the manner of Charley's untimely end, and wanting to forestall any more mayhem, performed a ritual wherein he called upon Charley to cease and desist if he had any ideas of retribution.

Charley is said to have appeared to the medicine man in quite a rage over his demise just when he was about to reap the rewards of conjugal bliss, and swore he would get even with his opponent. Thereupon the medicine man hurried to Charley's teepee to get the six-gun he'd owned. No sooner had he entered the empty dwelling than he was tripped and plunged full-length on the ground. At the same time, a heavy blanket was thrown over him, and a great weight held him down. He finally managed to extricate himself from the blanket, grabbed the gun, and left. Saddling up, he rode furiously for about five miles, dismantling the gun as he rode. Along the way he cast parts here and there, indiscriminately. Once during the ride he was literally pushed out of the saddle by the irate Charley, who knew full well what was going on and why it was being done. After the gun was distributed along the ride, the medicine man returned to the camp only to find his teepee burned to the ground and his goods scattered all over the place. He ritualed again, trying to reason with Charley, but apparently to no avail.

As the months went by the medicine man seemed to have lost his touch. He fell into such disrepute with the Indians he had to give up the practice and leave for parts unknown. The Indian who'd done poor Charley in didn't fare much better. He was thrown from his horse and broke his leg, his two cattle died from drinking poisoned water, and the girl skipped off with a brave from a neighboring tribe. Nothing more happened after that and everything returned to normal.

During that ride by the medicine man, when he was throwing parts of the gun around, another Indian out hunting observed where a piece of it landed and brought it back to his own teepee. When he found out it was Charley's, he kept quiet about it, hiding the evidence. That one piece was later broken down into two pieces—the brass butt and strap of the revolver, and the portion which had held the cylinder. These two remained in his family for two generations. The Indian who related the story is a great-grandson of the man who originally came by it. He exhibited the pieces to the postmaster of Cantil, California, Martin Engle, who has enjoyed the confidence of the Indians of the area for many years. Martin wrote down the serial number and sent back to the Colt Firearms Company in Hartford, Connecticut, for a rundown on it. Off to one side of the serial number, 7182, was the initial *K*, and under the number was the letter *A*. Colt returned the information that the weapon had been sold to Company A of the Texas Rangers, when Texas was still a territory. The initial *K* was for Kettering, the man who'd inspected it prior to its being sold to the rangers.

The Indian who owns the two pieces of the revolver still rides the trail between the old Indian camp where Charley lived, along the route taken by the medicine man when he was breaking the gun up and throwing the parts around. Many is the time during his ride when he hears the rush of wind past him, then it strikes the ground and raises huge dust clouds, rises again, then descends to raise another cloud of dust, as though someone is digging, sifting the sand, looking for something. It is believed by the Indians that Charley is still around trying to find the pieces of his revolver, although the object of Charley's revenge, the other Indian, is long gone, too—physically that is.

Let the White Man
Suffer

Indian lore, ghosts, and superstitions have been mostly handed down by word of mouth to each new generation. Thousands-of-years-old pictographs and petroglyphs have told some of the stories. Most fascinating of course is what the modern Indian believes today.

It isn't farfetched that a ghost could be assigned to remain at a certain place, accomplish a given mission for the mind who directed it—the subconscious mind has only memory and will continue doing what it has been directed after death. Such is the content of the following story as related to me by a Paiute Indian of the High Sierras, and who shall remain anonymous by request.

Around 1858 there was a good deal of activity by the U.S. military in the Mojave Desert, especially in the area of the towns of Mojave, Big Pine, Lone Pine, and Independence. The whites were making big mineral discoveries; prospectors from far and wide descended on the desert and mountains. With roving bands of pesky Indians getting in the way, as they tried to protect their land, the military was called on to supply troops while the whites encroached upon the red man's natural habitat.

Such a band of military was ambushed by a party of Indians who killed them all, then made off with their rifles, pistols, and supplies. (From what I've read in old military books, they had been issued the brand-new Colt rifle, model 1855, revolving cylinder, caliber 56, five-shot, percussion musket). The victorious braves tore back to the tribe, expecting to be greeted as heroes. Both the chief and the medicine man flipped! They knew that word of the massacre would get out, and if any warrior of theirs was to show up among the whites with such a military rifle it would be taken away from him, he would be immediately jailed, and probably summarily hanged.

After a hasty consultation it was decided the best thing to do was hide the evidence. The Indians rode out to a remote area and stashed the weapons in a small cave they knew of and covered it up. In addition, as with the kahunas of Hawaii, the medicine man performed his directed ritual of communicating with an excarnate subconscious mind. The spirit was charged to guard the hiding place, keep trespassers away if possible, and to let it be known if the cache was ever tampered with. The Indians of course firmly believe this, and respect it to this day. Time passed; the chief, the medicine man, and gradually most of the members of the tribe fell before the natural attrition of old age and physical death, but the word was handed down to succeeding generations.

Then, in 1967, an Indian showed up in Lone Pine, California, toting one of the old military rifles! He undoubtedly knew the whole story behind it, but he was also probably broke, and the rifle on today's market is worth in the neighborhood of from three to five hundred dollars. No sooner had he alighted from his beat up, old car than he was snatched up by five other Indians who hustled him off to their hogans outside of town.

According to my Indian informant, one of those Indians was psychic; he'd had a clairaudient visitation from the excarnate who'd been charged with guarding the cache, receiving word the rifle was on its way to Lone Pine. They loaded the miscreant into another car, and with others following took off for Jawbone Canyon, about fifty miles south of Lone Pine, where the rifle had been hidden. On the way they stopped four or five times, took the thief from the car, stripped him, and whipped him with creosote branches. When they arrived at Jawbone Canyon, they whipped him once again and turned him loose on foot with the final words for him to replace the rifle in its hiding place, destroy all evidence the cave had been tampered with, and then forget the whole matter.

It isn't known how many rifles, or other loot, are in the cave. When the cave is finally found and its contents brought to light, it will probably be done by a white man, perhaps a real estate developer having a hillside bulldozed for a housing development. The finders will rejoice on finding the stuff; an article will probably appear in a local newspaper about the lost hoard some U.S. troops no doubt placed there many years ago when the summer heat was so intense they couldn't pack it any further.

The Indians will smile knowingly amongst themselves and they will do some speculating. They didn't break the taboo. Let the white man suffer whatever is in store for him.

Lacking a written language until quite recently, there isn't much written material by the Indians about their ghosts and superstitions—sad, frustrating, but true. Even though the Indian is now attending high school and college (many entering business in large cities, basically he retains his culture, which is immersed in his own peculiar lore, as it should be.

Stripped of his land, herded into untenable reservations, shorn of his dignity, lied to, cheated, and suppressed, the Indian has managed to retain a rich heritage of ancestral pride, and lives in the presence of and is at peace with his natural spirits. It is difficult for the white man to get close enough to his Indian brother to promote a trustful revealing of Indian superstitions and ghosts. Therefore, when an Indian does divulge one of their secrets, it is well to listen and make notes, whether you think it is fact or fiction. To the teller, the legend is factual, and who is to gainsay? Their lore is as real to them as our Semitic Christ is to us: as real as the Bible is to the Christian with its fact and fiction; the Indian dates his beliefs back thousands of years before the coming of the white Messiah. Their beliefs are much simpler than what we've made of ours, too.

The Indians prayed to spirits of wind, storm, the hunt, the harvest; they believed in living spirits of the departed. They provided water, weapons, and food for a dead warrior on his trip to the other side, and were aware that not all those departees made the trip, but some hung around, sometimes for good, sometimes for evil purposes. As with the Hawaiian kahuna, or priest, some Indian medicine men have been on working terms with the spirits of departed warriors and have used those spirits to do their bidding. We've all heard the stories of fire walking performed by the Hawaiians, particularly over white-hot beds of lava, without burn or injury to the walker; how the Hawaiian Death Prayer is invoked against some individual who then begins to have the creeping paralysis that ends only with death, and who may not have had any idea of the prayer plot.

As we saw in the story of old MacSpreem, the subconscious mind, usually because of a violent death, continues to hang around, lacking direction of a conscious mind. It is held that the conscious mind of the kahuna, or the Indian medicine man, directs these excarnates to perform what we call primitive miracles. Christianity has supplanted these old beliefs and practices with new ones, complicated the whole concept, and thereby does not produce the visible evidences of the spirit world the Indians did—worse luck.

Just
a Friendly Visit

In contrast to stories of modern ghosts, I would like to introduce one about an excarnate Indian ghost who is undoubtedly *quite* old, judged by our earthly count of years.

One of my personal friends is an actor, an Indian, whom we shall call X. He costarred in the TV series "Yancy Derringer." Although X is a college graduate, a successful actor, owns property, and has business interests, he was delightfully open when I brought up the subject of ghosts—particularly of Indian lore and superstition regarding continuing life and the materialization of excarnates long dead.

As a public figure, X is a definite credit and assist to his people. He visits tribes all about the country, working for their welfare in any manner he can. One of his visits took him to the remnants of a tribe situated near San Diego, California. He had dinner one night with an Indian family that lives about a mile from an old Indian graveyard. X loves to listen to the lore of his people, and this is a story he learned from the San Diego family, to which each member will attest.

The family consists of husband, wife, and three children. The oldest child is a girl of fourteen. The children all attend the school which is about four miles from the house. The two younger children take the bus, but the fourteen-year-old has become a runner. She packs up her books and lunch, and trots the four miles each way, daily. On her return run from school one afternoon, as she was passing the graveyard, she looked over and saw what appeared to be a woman sitting atop one of the grave markers about one hundred feet from the road. She stopped to watch. The girl said she immediately knew what she was seeing, because the woman was sort of fuzzy, transparent, and she was dressed as Indians dressed in the old days: long braided hair, many beads around her neck, and coarse cloth, the skirt very long and elaborately stitched with colorful symbols. As she stood watching, the woman on the grave marker raised her head from the work she was doing with what looked like a basket, and smiled at her.

This being the first time the girl had ever encountered an excarnate, and, although she was raised on the belief in them, she was scared and she took off for home at a full run. Bursting into the house she told her folks what she'd seen, and they all piled into the family car and drove back to the graveyard. The old woman had disappeared. Since it was now believed a spirit was around, close, the father decided to drive the kids to school and back himself, in the hope that when they passed the graveyard they might see the woman. They did. On Tuesday afternoon of the following week, as they were all driving past the graveyard, there she was, sitting atop the same grave marker. The father and the kids got out of the car and stood in the road, watching her. The woman smiled at them, then waved! They waved back. The girl ran over and vaulted the fence, wanting to get as close as possible, but with that, the woman vanished.

The wife then began accompanying them on the drive to and from school, and she too saw the woman; in fact, on one day, the wife saw her first. They have not been able to get closer than about fifty feet before the woman disappears, but always there are smiles and waves exchanged between them. Unfortunately, there is no name on the old marker. They don't know why the woman chose that particular spot to materialize, but there she is, and is seen by at least one member of the family practically every day or so. Once they placed some food on the marker, but when they checked the next morning, it was untouched. That afternoon as they drove back from the school house, there she was, sitting on the marker, smiling and waving. It is frustrating to all of them that they can't talk with her, but that's the way it is sometimes when dealing with those on the "other side." They can be as frustrating and contrary as we mortals!

Jesse Came Back

The precursors of our modern-day occult and spiritistic thinking are our ancestors from the Stone Age, early dabblers in witchcraft, the shamans, and the Indian medicine men. It is difficult, if not at times impossible, for modern man to admit to empiricals and veridicals that are thousands of years old. What one generation believed, the next might not; they must be shown. And living in the materialistic age hasn't elevated man's spiritual or occult thinking to the level of his scientific knowledge until quite recently; now, having sated himself with those scientific advances that enable him with a flick of a switch to destroy all earthly life, he has come to the realization that there still remains "something" within man which scientific analysis is unable to define or account for. So far this something has eluded us, but we are getting close. It is called the God concept, or Higher Power. Some races and societies believe more than others, but the evidence is there, and mounting.

As has been aforementioned, it is difficult to get stories from the Indians. They guard their lore and superstition jealously, and with good reason; they've often been the butt of ridicule and persecution at the hands of the white man since they were subdued. It is therefore with gratitude that I pass on to you the following which was related by the loving couple who adopted a half-caste Indian-Negro boy, raised him as their own, saw him go off to war in Vietnam, and finally, attended his military funeral.

Roy Higgins and his wife, the foster parents, live in Bridgeport, California, in a small, frame house squatted at the south end of the airport runway used by sportsmen. The house is just across the road from the area occupied by what is left of the local Indian tribe. This tribe has remained in spite of the rigor of their lives, trying to make a living in a white community where they are still not wholly accepted. They are photographed during the tourist season as oddities.

The Higgins adopted their foster son, Jesse, when he was a tiny baby. The natural mother died, and the little outcaste was up for grabs and would have ended up in an orphanage for Indians and children from mixed marriages if it had not been for these people. They had no children of their own and welcomed the responsibility.

Jesse attended as much schooling as is provided locally, then enrolled in extension courses administered by colleges in Los Angeles. He applied himself diligently to anything he undertook, and was well thought of among both the white and the Indian populations.

When he was in his middle teens, an outside room was added to the south end of the small, frame dwelling for him. Although Jesse's room was attached to the house, it wasn't possible to include it as an integral part of the building, and so he had his own outside door. In order to get into the house from Jesse's room, it was necessary for him to walk down the side of the house, past the kitchen window, and come around the building. The main entrance was the kitchen door.

At age nineteen he was drafted into the Army, received his basic and advanced training, and was then shipped to Vietnam. The folks heard from him every ten or twelve days, receiving the usual post cards, souvenirs, and personal mementos most servicemen and women send back to their families. He seemed quite happy; his letters were always enthusiastic about his work and the men in his outfit; he felt very sorry about the condition of the South Vietnamese civilians.

The last letter, which I read, was dated August 1968. Then, as his foster mother said, there was silence. Two weeks after that last letter arrived, she was standing in the kitchen one morning making breakfast. A movement caught her eye and she looked out the window. Jesse was passing by the window! It surprised her, but she immediately thought perhaps he had gotten leave, arrived home in the middle of the night, and hadn't wanted to disturb them. She went to the kitchen door, opened it, and stepped out to greet him. Jesse did not appear. She walked around the house calling his name. There was no answer. Roy Higgins, who had gone the few blocks into Bridgeport, returned as she was walking around outside, and she told him of seeing Jesse. They both went to his room. Nothing was disturbed, there was no evidence that anyone had occupied it since he left.

The following morning, at about the same time, the couple were in the kitchen having breakfast when Jesse again passed by the window; they both saw him simultaneously. They went to the door and opened it, expecting to see him. Not there. The Indians have a superstition borne out by centuries of experience, and that is, when an Indian dies, he will usually make one or two visits to the family or other members of the tribe, just to let them know he is still around, then depart for the "happy hunting ground." The two were convinced Jesse was dead, and they waited for some word.

A week after the two sightings, a lieutenant and a sergeant from the official notifying office in Los Angeles made a call to inform them that Jesse had been killed in action in Vietnam on a date that preceded his appearance in Bridgeport by one day. His body was being flown home, and the military wanted to conduct the full military burial, honor guard, rifle salute and all. They told the two military men they already knew of his death, and I can imagine the subsequent reaction. When they told them Jesse had passed by the window twice the day after his death, their consternation must have been complete. Most whites don't dig Indian superstition; nor can they explain it!

Jesse was buried up there, in Bridgeport, with the full military honors. Over two hundred Indians and whites attended the services for this boy who had done his best as an adopted son and later as a soldier in the service of a government whose people had stripped both Indian and Negro of their dignity.

Upon his death, Jesse fulfilled the last earthly mission of his people—returning to those who loved him, and whom he loved, to let them know of his continuing life. Thank you, Jesse. And thank you Mr. and Mrs. Roy Higgins for allowing me to tell the story.

Three
Little Indians

California Highway Patrolman Ben Anderson and I were having coffee in a restaurant near Lone Pine on the evening of March 29, 1970. We'd been swapping ghost stories from around the state when Ben remembered one that came from the Paiute Indians in Lone Pine. (Ben gave all the names of the individuals, but to keep faith with those who wished to remain anonymous, I have changed the true names of all participants, except for that of Dr. Christiansen.)

An Indian family named Cutler lived on the outskirts of Lone Pine. It was a large family consisting of Mr. Cutler, his wife Nora, and their eight children, but by 1964 only three of the younger ones were still living at home: Harold, age five; Cole, nine; and Rick, fourteen.

Mr. Cutler had given Rick an old rifle, in good working order, and the boy prized it highly. He was admonished time and again not to leave it around where the two younger ones could get it, but if he's like most boys with a gun of his own, it would have been jealously guarded and protected anyhow. Rick usually kept the gun on top of a portable clothes closet in his bedroom. The gun was never loaded until Rick had left the house and seldom before he arrived at the area where he was going hunting. Now we get into a chain of events.

That particular day in 1964, Rick had taken the gun down from the top of the closet. He said he didn't remember loading it, left it on the bed while he went out to the barn to do some chores. Before leaving he warned both Harold and Cole, who were in the house at the time, not to touch it, and they promised they wouldn't. Like most boys, a loose gun lying around is an open invitation to inspect it, especially if they'd been told not to.

The two boys were now alone in the house. Mr. and Mrs. Cutler were working out in the garden. Suddenly there was a shot from within the house. The parents and Rick quickly ran inside and found Cole standing with the rifle in his hands, Harold was lying on the floor with a bullet through the head. Harold had died instantly.

Rick grabbed the gun away from Cole; Mr. Cutler ran for a phone and called Dr. Don Christiansen in Lone Pine. Mrs. Cutler went into a state of shock when she couldn't revive Harold. Dr. Christiansen arrived in short order, and pronounced Harold dead. Then the constable was called, and he, too, arrived in a few minutes. Cole denied from the outset that he'd shot Harold, and no amount of questioning, threatening, or pleading could shake his story.

Under questioning by the constable, Cole's constant remark was, "I didn't do it. I picked the gun up, and then something swung me around, and then it went off, but I didn't do it. Somebody else did it."

Cole was sorry his brother was dead, but he felt no guilt or remorse because "somebody else did it." Cole continues to this day to say and believe that he didn't do the firing, and perhaps with good cause.

Mrs. Cutler was put to bed in a state of shock. Dr. Christiansen administered a strong sedative which allowed her to mercifully escape into sleep. Of course the word went out around their circle of friends and relatives about the tragedy, and some of them gathered at the Cutler home.

Sometime later that evening, Nora slept off the sedative and awakened. Everyone was fearful of the outcome. Nora was vaguely aware of her friends in the room, but seemed completely withdrawn, ignoring any food offered her or showing any signs of interest or recognition.

Finally they heard her say something. Going to the bed, they leaned over and asked her if she was all right. She murmured, "Do you see the little people?"

Nora was looking toward the foot of the bed, and they asked her where they were. "There, on the foot of my bed."

"What are they doing?"

"They are laughing and dancing. They are very happy."

"Who are they?"

"They are three little Indians." (She raised her hand indicating they were about three inches in height). "There are two men and a woman."

The others looked but could see nothing, and of course it was decided she was "seeing things" because of the shock or Dr. Christiansen's sedative. Nora remained conscious and awake until nearly midnight, and all the time her attention was riveted to the three little Indians. Then she slept again.

The relatives present, in addition to Rick and Cole, included an aunt, an uncle, Mrs. Cutler's sister Hattie, and a long-time friend of the family, Morris. They all remained in the house overnight. Mr. Cutler didn't arrive home from the constable's office until after two in the morning. Cole was not held, officially, of course, but they wanted to question him at more length.

At eight o'clock the following morning Mrs. Cutler was

still asleep, and the others, having had breakfast, were seated on the front porch, making plans for the funeral. The sister, Hattie, said, "There comes a car. It must be Dr. Christiansen."

The approaching vehicle was a blue pickup truck. Morris, who knew Dr. Christiansen's car, said, "It's not Dr. Christiansen, he doesn't drive a pickup."

The truck stopped on the street in front of the house and a man and woman got out. The man was dressed in a flat-topped black hat, black shirt, blue jeans, and black cowboy boots, and was carrying a long package wrapped in brown paper. The group remained on the porch as the couple came up the walk. The man spoke first, "This is the Cutler house. Did my little people arrive?"

Morris told me that at that moment his hair felt like it stood straight up and grew another inch! I guess everyone was so dumbfounded they couldn't speak, because Morris asked the questions. "What do they look like?"

"They are about three inches high (indicating). Two men and a woman."

"How did you know about them?"

"I sent them. I knew there was trouble here, and I sent them on ahead to be with Mrs. Cutler until I could arrive."

"Who are you?"

"I'm a medicine man. I am an Indian."

"Where are you from?"

"I live in Utah. My wife and I drove all night to be here this morning." The medicine man went on to tell that he had received "word" psychicly, that there had been a fatality in the Cutler family, and so he and his wife had driven some four hundred miles from Utah across Nevada and into California.

"No, we were not called by telephone. We don't have a telephone where we live."

Finally the medicine man said, "There is one here among you who does not believe. That one is bad for what we have to do, and I ask that one to leave, now."

The four looked at each other, and then Nora's sister, Hattie, stood up and said that she was the one who didn't believe, and would not believe. She turned and left them, returning to her own home.

The medicine man, without revealing what was in the package, invited all the relatives and Morris to come back that night for the service he would perform—which *must* be performed. After requesting they be left alone with Mrs. Cutler, he and his wife then entered the house. Morris, the only nonrelative, felt the service was a family affair. He departed, and did not attend that night.

The following day Morris talked with one of the relatives who'd been present at the "service." The package the medicine man carried was an eagle's wing. Morris didn't know what its significance is, except that it is a symbol of power. The medicine man performed his rites using the wing to sweep out the evil discarnate spirit who had caused young Cole to take the rifle and shoot his brother. During the ceremony, which lasted most of the night, the medicine man and the evil spirit went round and round. The eagle's wing was forcibly jerked from his hands a number of times. The spirit "grabbed" the wing and pulled the man across the room, hurling him against the wall. After many hours the exorcism rite was complete, the spirit seemingly running out of power. After sailing an aluminum frying pan across the room and belting the medicine man over the left eye with it, the spirit left.

The following day, little Harold was buried in the cemetery in Independence, California. After the interment, Mrs. Cutler was riding back home with Morris and Mr. Cutler, and she asked if they had seen the eagle flying above her car on the way to the cemetery. They hadn't, but she elaborated on the description, how it hovered near her, looking at her with kind eyes, its wings brushing her, protecting her from possible return of the evil spirit, or any other passing spirit who might have tried to cause trouble.

The medicine man remained in Lone Pine for about a week, holding counsel for the Indians, and according to my informant of this phase, performed some pretty paranormal feats, such as healing the sick and the lame.

Psychiatry has a ball with cases like this. They would begin with the premise that Cole has suffered from a conscious, or subconscious sibling jealousy, that when the opportunity presented itself, he "accidentally" shot and killed Harold. Harold was the youngest, he'd taken the cherished place of attention Cole had previously enjoyed from all members of the family.

As for the three little Indians on the foot of Mrs. Cutler's bed, there are many people who've been committed to mental institutions for insisting on having seen or experienced similar phenomena. Only recently, in the past seventy years, with the advent of the science of parapsychology, has the occult—extra sensory perception, clairvoyance, clairaudience, etc.—begun to come into its own. Psychiatrists are less quick to commit a person to a fidget farm who has seen apparitions, or heard voices. Some things, such as the psychic phenomena we are learning about by leaps and bounds, are indemonstrable. Investigation and research reveal the study is as deep as it is wide.

The medicine man is quite obviously a psychic of what we must call high order. His receiving of the word of the tragedy at almost the time it happened, knowing to whom, and where, it happened, sending his "little people" to be with Mrs. Cutler, all bear loud and clear paranormal testimony to the immediate and constant knowledge and informative interpenetration the spirit world has with us physical earthlings. We've come a long way (baby), and we've got a long way to go to even scratch the surface of what we *don't* know.

Spiritual Photography

"It's Lonely, Being Ghostly!"

The large recorder was on, the tape was running through. There was no sound except a hum. Then suddenly there was a "pop," and I heard what sounded like, "Art, this is dad." Quick. That was it. Then the hum resumed.

"What was that?" I asked the man operating the machine. He turned it off.

"That's my dad. He comes through quite frequently. So does my brother, Edson. Listen to it again." He reversed the tape, then ran it forward. "Art, this is dad."

Art is Attila Von Szalay. Professionally, he is a photographer with the Harold Hall Portrait Gallery, in Van Nuys, California. Privately, he is a psychic (sensitive to nonphysical forces). He is also a medium (a substance through which a force acts or an effect is transmitted). I was interviewing Attila because I'd heard he took what are called Spirit Photographs and was in touch with ghosts. So "they" said. The tape recording of discarnate voices was an added surprise. You never know just what will happen when you visit psychically gifted people. (Sometimes even they don't know what will happen!)

"Attila, you've been in California, particularly the Hollywood area, for some time, haven't you?"

"About thirty years, yes."

"I've heard and read about you."

"Yes, every once in awhile something really startling shows up in my pictures, some manifestation that gets me into the news, then they have me on TV."

"When did you have your first experience with spirit photography? When you filmed your first spirit?"

"It was around 1940. I was working for Eastern Columbia, at Broadway and Ninth before that in 1938. They fired me because the film I was handling came out splotched, with light streaks on it. They just thought I was careless. Then in 1940 I began doing photography myself. The first spirit photograph, if you can call it that, was one I made of a woman. It shows starlike lights around the area of her spleen. That was the beginning. Eastern Columbia did me a favor when they fired me."

"When did spirit photography begin? Who first noted it?" (Usually I think of the deep, searching questions *after* I've had the session with a person!)

"It was discovered, or invented, whichever you prefer, in 1838. Twenty-three years later the first spirit photograph was made by an engraver named Mumler, in Boston. When he took photographs of his friends, the plate showed the impression of other people. Thousands of spirit photographs have been taken since then, and a majority of them have been verified by scientific researchers as authentic."

"Attila, my next question has to be, 'Is the sitter the medium for the pictures, or is it the photographer?' "

"It can be either one, but usually it's the photographer. When the sitter and the photographer are both mediums, then you can get some really startling pictures."

I noticed Attila would frequently pick up one particular

photo, then lay it down. "Attila, what other pictures have you made that have been verified as spirit photography?" (And that was just what he wanted me to ask!)

"The most famous one, is the picture I took which became known as the NAD/Kelly case. Miss Michaela Kelly came to me in 1952 as a volunteer for a hypnosisfilm experiment. I photographed her while she was hynotized. When the picture was developed it was found to contain a spirit 'extra' who wore a shawl. In large print were the letters *N A D*.

"When Miss Kelly returned to normal she was asked if the letters on the figure had any significance to her. She finally remembered that there had been a housekeeper who worked at her house many years ago whose name was Naddie. The housekeeper had died fourteen and a half years previously. Miss Kelly underwent a lie detector test on a TV show called "Lie Detector." The result of the test proved conclusively, for the first time in history, really, that spirit photography was a reality. That raised a ruckus in scientific circles for a long time, but they could not disprove it."

Now we were really launched, and I wanted to get as much material as I could—get all his "spooky" stories if possible. Since he's had so many photographic manifestations, spirits on film, I had to ask if there were any more that were checked out as authentic?

He smiled. "Many times. I'm the heavy in these things, especially when someone comes for a sitting expecting to get a spirit on film. There are times when people just come in to have a portrait made, and spirits show up on the film with them. In answer to your question, yes, there is another incident which ultimately checked out, although when it was verified very little space was given it.

"In 1952, a dentist and an auto dealer took off in an airplane in an Idaho snow storm, and they were never heard from again. The wife of one of them was brought to me by a gypsy fortune-teller she'd gone to, who practiced in Hollywood. The gypsy had heard I made spirit photographs, and asked if I could get a picture of the missing husband if the wife sat for me? I said of course not, I'm only an experimentalist, I'm glad to get a configuration, not get anything of a veridical nature. She whispered to me to at least try, just to make the woman feel better. I said all right, why not. So we went into the studio, and I made a half-dozen pictures. When I developed them, I'd gotten this configuration showing a horseshoe, with the number 5, and what looks like a man sitting in the fuselage of a plane without wings; and water, and so on. A reporter got hold of the story, and he wrote it up, even giving the names [I have them deleted], and the woman didn't like that. Her lawyer called me up and raised the devil because I'd even taken the photos.

"After I developed the picture I said let's get a map of Idaho and try to find something in relation to the horseshoe and the number 5. We did. Sophia Williams (now deceased) that great psychometrist [one who divines facts about an object or its owner through contact with, or proximity to, the object] who lived right across the street from me in the Old Park Hotel in Hollywood in the 1930s, came over and said that the gypsy woman had come to her the day before with the woman, and she knew they'd been to see me, and what did I find?

"I asked her what she got psychometrizing for the woman. She named a place in Idaho. Then I got out the map, and I said, 'O.K., I got what I think would be a horseshoe.' I showed her on the map where I thought the plane with the men was downed. It was Horseshoe Bend, Idaho, with the number 5 printed right below it on a road, indicating mileage between two points. It coincided to within five or ten miles of the place she'd given me. So both of us got the general area. She did it by psychometry, I did it with spirit photography. The spirit of the woman's husband could manifest on the film because of the mediumistic gift I have. About two years later some hunters were in that area and they found the plane with the two skeletons in it, which were later identified as the dentist and the car dealer. The most interesting thing about this case, *only* the two men knew where they were, no one else, otherwise they could have been found.

"No living person knew where the men were. They were killed in the wreck, which would rule out telepathy between living minds in a physical body. An article did appear in a Hollywood newspaper, but it was only a small one, and they didn't mention that either Sophia Williams or Attila Von Szalay had come up with an approximate location of the plane, two years earlier. They would rather forget they had laughed at us."

As Attila finished the story he had gotten up and was moving quite definitely toward the door of the partition separating the display room of the studio from the photographic sitting room where he took his spirit photographs. I followed, naturally, because this was a fascinating man, and I wanted to be in on anything which he might produce, apport, conjure, or whatever! I'm game.

The room contained all the paraphernalia for his picture work, and in addition, sitting on a table in the rear was the recording machine I mentioned at the beginning of this story, where I came in. He busied himself setting up a tripod and mounting a flash camera on it. When the camera suited him, he had me sit in a chair about eight feet out in front of it.

Placing the end of a long cord, attached to the camera, in my hand, explaining that he would get everything in readiness, then come and stand beside me. When I "cocked" the trigger on the gadget on the end of the cord, and then spoke, my voice would set off the camera. When he developed the pictures we would see if anyone "else" was in them, or what.

Being me, I would probably work in reverse of Ted Serios, of the thoughtographic eyes; when I spoke and set the camera off, a spirit would come *out* of the lens! It didn't happen that way, much as I would have liked it. Attila stood beside me, and said, "Anytime." I cocked the trigger, then said, "Is anyone here with us?" The camera went off with a brilliant flash. Four such pictures were taken.

I must digress here, take us forward a few days. Attila called to tell me that three of the shots were of just the two of us, the other one showed me as being my good old solid self, but he was almost transparent. He couldn't give any explanation for the phenomenon, but swore he didn't do it himself. He pointed out that the way the two of us were integrated in the shot any hanky-panky was precluded.

Now back to the Tape Recorder Session as I call it. It's Attila doing the talking. "As far as people on the other side being close to me—and I'm talking about receiving messages on the tape recorder—we can sit here in full daylight, as we are now, and you can hold the mike in any position you want to, and hopefully we'll get an answer to a question, or some little whispers. Wouldn't that indicate I'm surrounded by what people call ghosts?" His grin was impish.

He went on. "Or, we can turn the machine on, go out, lock the door and go two doors away, or three, whichever, and still get the answers to my questions. Not your questions, mine, unless I ask them for you. I've asked questions when I was in a building up the street, and gotten answers here on the machine.

"Now, there is always the possibility of fraud being produced by having someone with a walkie-talkie, someone sitting across the street with one, and a little transceiver here in the room, but you eliminate that by bugging the place, or, getting a Faraday Cage. The Faraday Cage was constructed to inhibit radio waves, among other things. So, I've clambered inside the Faraday Cage under test conditions, and I've still produced the voices, or rather, those who work through and with me from the other side produce them.

"A magazine writer insisted that I sit in the dark, and I asked him what could be accomplished by that? I could produce fraud in the dark a lot easier than I could in the daylight. We did it both ways, to suit him, and he was convinced, after many trials. I would rather do it out in the open, where everyone can watch. I've got nothing to hide.

"Even if the quality is not good that we get on the tape, we do get a supernatural voice. Now, whether it is the person claiming to be familiar with the Sharon Tate murder case, or my son, I can't *prove* it. Even if there is someone on the other side impersonating them, the ones in the Tate case, the main thing is there *is* someone there to impersonate. A supernormal voice does exist, there is intelligence; man survives death, and he can communicate under certain conditions. But this is not for the spiritualists. They get big, round pear-shaped tones in the dark, and they will not submit to lie detector tests of any kind, you see. So, I would rather have a little, tiny, miniscule voice. Those people on the other side are *dead* as far as we are concerned. Where being dead is, nobody knows, but the mere fact they can communicate with us is phenomenal."

I broke in here. "Attila, have you ever asked questions about the Tate murder case?"

"Yes. I've gotten answers from 'someone' over there who professes to be one of the group in the case, but I can't *prove* it."

"Have you ever asked those who work with you on the other side what it is like 'over there?'"

"Most mediums have, and the best answer I can give you from what I've received—it is different, but not that different. They are in an altered state of consciousness. They are more keenly aware than we are; distance doesn't exist for them, nor time. Until they move on to a higher plane, or another altered plane of consciousness, they seem to be about as earthbound as we are. It would seem we are down at the bottom of the fishbowl here on earth, in our physical bodies."

Now it was time to see some of this discarnate contact possibly come through on the tape recorder. "Do you believe 'they,' your contacts, or whomever, are present, right here with us, like now?"

He smiled, and his eyes were alert to catch either skepticism, or nervousness at the thought of being surrounded by spooks. "I think so, yes. Let's try for another voice. Maybe we'll get one, maybe not."

He switched on the recorder, and while it was warming up, handed me a sealed box containing one thousand feet of quarter-inch Concord recording tape. "Check it. You tell me if it's been opened?"

I looked it over carefully. It seemed to be in the condition to which the company had brought it when it was sealed and shipped. "You open it and give it to me."

I broke the seal, opened the box, slid out the tape, looked

it over, and handed it to him. He threaded it into the machine, handed me the microphone, and had me place some headphones over my ears, told me that if and when I heard, or thought I heard something besides the high hum of the machine turned full up to signal him and he would stop the machine, run it back and see if we'd picked up something. We began. About a third of the tape had run through the recording head, and suddenly there was a definite *pop,* and a jumble of "something" which sounded like very rapid whispering. I signaled. Attila stopped the tape, ran it back. I took off the headphones. He played the tape forward—there was the *pop*— then the quickly whispered words, "Art, this is Edson, how are you?" He ran it back and played it again, then again.

I've not gone into these ghost stories to either prove or disprove. I'm reporting them as they were related to me, or how I experienced them, but I will say that during the time the tape was running through the machine, prior to the *pop* and the words, I hadn't taken my eyes off Attila. His lips never moved, his throat didn't convulse, even slightly, because the thought occurred to me that he might be a ventriloquist. Nothing.

"Now what do you think?" he asked.

"Well, it's there, that's for sure. Do you have other tapes of Edson speaking to you?"

He got up, riffled through the stack of boxes, drew one out, opened it, took out the tape, took the other tape off the machine, and threaded the new one into it. Turning it on, we sat and listened. The *pop* occurred—the same voice said, "Go to the doctor. This is Edson." Attila turned it off, and said, "Why should I have gone to the doctor? I felt fine. The next day I came down with what was diagnosed as pleurisy pneumonia. I'd had no indication of anything in the chest, no cold. But Edson knew it and was trying to warn me." He reached over and turned the machine on. "Listen to this."

There was the familiar hum for some time, then it *popped*—"Hot dogs, Art, ha, ha." It was definitely a feminine voice, light, gay.

"Who was that?"

"When I was a young photographer I used a beautiful girl as my model and she loved hot dogs. Anytime we were going out anyplace she would always ask, "Hot dogs, Art?" then laugh. We finally made a pact—whichever one passed over first would try to make contact with the other—something about Hot Dogs. It took me some time to hook it up, remember it, but there she is. She's never come through with anything but that, maybe just to let me know she's around."

"Has she passed on? Do you know if she's on the other side?"

"No, I've never checked. It's been so long ago. I wouldn't know where to begin."

From my own contact with psychics and mediums around the country, it's been my observation they are in the main people apart. They are lionized, eulogized, and ferociously used by many. This was an excellent opportunity to get another opinion. "Attila, do you have something of a problem with people? I mean, knowing you are psychic, how do people act and react to you?"

"Some people accept it, believe it; some, most I would say, are rather skeptical, they want to be shown and shown; then there are lots of them who avoid me, call me a spook, or a kook, get angry with me, order me out, even. They don't want me near them, or particularly they don't want me to touch them." He smiled, ruefully. "Sometimes it's lonely, being known as ghostly."

That last I could well understand. I get somewhat the same treatment being an actor! Sought after, pursued, used, but always there is that separateness, as though the users, the seekers, were standing off from you. I've been with groups occasionally who actually surround you, then one of them will say, "Act." I'm an actor, so I act. Psychics are supposed to perform on command or be very suspect as frauds. "Bring Uncle Harry, now."

"One last question, Attila. Do you think you are, let's say, surrounded by ghosts, departed spirits, all the time, or do they know they can manifest through you and come to you when they want to bring information?"

He pondered this for a moment. "I think those on the other side know which people in the physical body are capable of being used as mediums for their expression. I don't know when some discarnate will manifest through me, but, yes, I do think they are aware of me, and others like me, so that would indicate they are rather close, or, they can move pretty fast and get to me when it's necessary."

I'd seen a lot, I'd learned a lot from Attila Von Szalay. We'd been together four hours, and it passed rather like one hour. No doubt a book could be written about him, and probably will be one day. As I pulled away from the curb I looked back and waved. Attila waved, and I thought, "He is different. He could very well be misunderstood. It must be mighty lonely, being ghostly."

If you're ever in Van Nuys, California, in the San Fernando Valley, look up Attila Von Szalay at the Harold Hall Studios, get your portrait made. You might be surprised at *who* might appear with you!

Noncommittal
Ghosts

A Lake Tahoe
Ghost

Lake Tahoe is a jewel of California/Nevada. Part of it is in California, part in Nevada. You can gamble on one side of the lake, not on the other. Mark Twain wrote of Lake Tahoe: "A noble sheet of blue water lifted six thousand, three hundred feet above the level of the sea, and walled in by a rim of snow-clad mountain peaks that towered aloft a full three thousand feet higher still! It was a vast oval, and one would have to use up eighty or a hundred good miles in traveling around it. As it lay there with the shadows of the mountains brilliantly photographed upon its still surface I thought it must surely be the fairest picture the whole earth affords."

The vast oval looked the same as we flew over it for a landing on its still surface. That is, the same, with the addition of the debris and civilized fouling we humans set out the moment we touch a new place. The second night Twain and his partner stayed at the lake, even they accidentally started a huge fire that burned for four hours, destroying their camp and acres and acres of manzanita, chapparal, and pine trees. Aside from an occasional trapper or prospector, there were no inhabitants at Lake Tahoe then; they came later.

One of those later inhabitants moved onto the shore of Lake Tahoe about twenty-two years ago. The man, his wife, and their three children had the house built by carpenters from Carson City, Nevada, that most interesting town down the mountain from them. They lived there all year 'round. The house was only two hundred feet back from the water, facing it.

It isn't known exactly when the husband and father went fishing in his small boat, capsized and sank to oblivion, in a depth reputed to be over fifteen hundred feet. As far as the man who related the narrative can remember, it happened about seven years after the family moved in. The boat was found, but neither the body, nor clothes, nor any gear ever came to light.

One evening, just at dusk, about a month after the disappearance, the wife and the children were sitting on the front porch of the house, looking out over the lake. Suddenly, Annalie, the second daughter, pointed and said, "Look, that looks like dad!"

The others followed the direction of her pointed finger. Walking along the water's edge was a man dressed in a slouch straw hat, vest, shirt, and baggy trousers. Annalie darted from the porch and ran down toward the figure, her sister and brother following her. The mother remained motionless, unbelieving. As Annalie got to within some twenty-five feet of the figure, it disappeared, just vanished. The children gathered in a group and stood there, looking about, calling in all directions. There was no answer, and the apparition didn't reappear. When they got back to the porch, they asked their mother if she'd seen "dad."

"Yes, I saw—something. It looked like a man walking. It couldn't have been your father."

"It was dad!"

"If it was dad, he would have seen us. He would have come to us."

There was "spirited" conversation all during dinner that evening. The two older children took a powerful lamp and returned to the spot where they had seen the figure, but they looked in vain. The next morning they again went to the water's edge and looked for footprints, or some evidence there had been someone there. Nothing. Within the next two weeks the ghostly figure was seen almost every other night, just at dusk, at about the same time period the authorities gave to the mishap which took the man's life.

Once word was out it caused a good deal of furore around the lake, people descending on the area to see if they could get a look at the ghost. It always appeared at about the same place, walked about a hundred feet, then disappeared. Two men drove a long pole into the ground ten feet out from shore and strung a heavy line to a tree fifty feet from the water. Then they watched as the figure made its walk *right through the line,* not cutting or moving it, or disturbing it in any manner.

Two archeology students who lived in Carson City heard about the apparition and brought infrared lamps and a camera. When the figure was seen moving along the water's edge, they snapped on the light and took three photos in rapid succession. What appeared on the developed film was a transparency of the figure of a man—dim, indistinct, but definitely the outline of a human being.

The family had become so upset by the continuing trauma of having literally dozens of people descending upon them with questions and new ways to "trap" the ghost that they finally sold the house and property and moved to Los Angeles.

That was about fifteen years ago. I talked with eleven people, all of whom swear they have seen the "dead" man at least twice in the past year. The four days we spent there, watching for him ourselves, were fruitless, and we had to give it up. It doesn't seem there is any particular time of year, or month, he appears, but according to the people of Lake Tahoe, he *does* return to the spot where he launched his row boat on the last physical journey he took in this life.

Is this manifestation one of continuing memory of the departed spirit, wherein he knows what he is doing? Why does he walk the beach for those few feet then disappear? Why didn't he acknowledge the presence of his loved ones? Or, does the spot contain the memory of the man walking on the beach, getting into his boat? Is the memory tape of time replaying, time after time?

The one conclusion we come to is this: "In the depths of man there lie indications of life and faculties not limited to a planetary existence of this material world." From my own ghostly investigations, which cover a number of years, I feel completely comfortable with and proceed on the supposition that there is a spirit world where those of us departed still exist, perhaps as real as the one we are in, and they are right here in our midst.

"Mommie, Speak to Me"

Ghost stories are contributed heavily by the Alabama Hills right outside Lone Pine, California. There isn't any explanation for the wealth of phenomena in that area, but my research shows more stories from around there, and Bridgeport, and Bodie, than from any other area in the Sierra Nevadas.

As told by Earl Richardson: "A man named George lived in those Alabama Hills some years ago. He's dead now, of natural causes. He and his wife, Adele, had two little children at the time of her death. Adele was a hardy Georgia cracker girl, from the deep back country, where the red clay is abundant and unyielding, where the folks scratch mightily for a bare living. No one knows where George came from, he never told me, but he and Adele had been married for about five years; moved to the Alabamas a year before the first child was born.

"The house they built was a three-room affair, a shack: parlor, bedroom, and kitchen. They lived in real poverty. The oldest boy was four, the youngest two and a half when Adele passed on. George not only couldn't pay her medical bills, he built her coffin with his own hands. The neighbors came over and helped 'lay her out.' The coffin was placed in the parlor, with Adele in it. George and the children were alone in the kitchen. The kids had gone to sleep lying on some blankets near the stove as it was pretty cool outside. George was pondering what in the world to do with them, as he worked a mining claim about one and a half miles from the house and was gone from early morning until usually after dark.

"Suddenly he heard a noise, or sound, from the front parlor, and looking up saw Adele approaching through the doorway. She was fully dressed, in the clothes he'd laid her out in. He spoke to her but she paid him no attention. She walked over to the stove and stood looking down at the sleeping children, then she bent over and put out her hand like she was going to touch them, but didn't. She remained bent over, looking at them for a moment or two. George didn't move out of his chair, but called her name a couple of times, got no response or notice from her. Then Adele stood up, looked at George, smiled, and disappeared.

"The next day, around noon, the same thing happened, except this time when Adele appeared, walking into the kitchen from the parlor, the oldest boy saw her, also. He didn't try to go to her, but talked to her. 'Mommie, I thought you went away. See I'm eating my sandwich.'

"Adele smiled at him, walked over and stood close beside the other child who was unaware of her, and he asked, 'Where is Mommie?' The oldest boy pointed to her and said, 'There.'

" 'I don't see her.'

" 'She's right there, aren't you, Mommie?'

"Adele merely smiled.·

"George was witness to all this. He thought he'd been having hallucinations the previous day when she appeared, but this time he knew he wasn't. Adele stayed only a few moments, then disappeared. It took some doing for George to explain to the older boy how his mother could be in the coffin, dead, and how she could be walking around the house!

"After the funeral the next day, the three of them returned to the house, and I went with them. The few people who'd attended the service had brought along some food which they left with George, and which he was serving to the kids.

"George was getting some plates from the cupboard, the kids were sitting at the table with me. All at once, the older boy looked up in the direction of the parlor and said, 'Mommie!' I can tell you I was scared. I hollered to George that she was here. I got up and went over near the outside door, as I didn't know what was going to happen. George put down the pan he had and looked toward the parlor. He called her name, but I didn't hear any answer.

"George said she went over to the table and just stood there, looking at the kids. The oldest boy always saw her, and said, 'Mommie, why don't you speak to me? Are you in the ground?' I guess kids don't get scared at things like that like we older folks do. George said that Adele just smiled, looking at them, then she disappeared. The boy got up and called for her. Frankly, I didn't want to stay around there. I left. George told me that every day for a week after the funeral Adele was still coming back, sometimes during the day, sometimes at night. The kids were getting pretty upset, the bigger one because he could see her and she wouldn't talk to him, the smaller one because he couldn't see her, and he kept crying for her.

"After that week, George said that she stopped coming and he hadn't seen her anymore. He gave the kids to a brother of his who lived near Bakersfield, California, and moved higher into the Alabamas, nearer his mining claim. He dug a cave in that sandstone formation you can see from Portal Road as you go up to Mt. Whitney, and lived all by himself, just working his mine.

"He didn't seem to change any, except he got dirtier and dirtier, and looked more like a pack rat than a human being. He would come down to my house once in awhile and tell me that Adele had visited him. In fact, he said that some relatives, including his father and mother, had come to him, and they even had conversations. I stayed away from his cave, and everyone else did too. It became known as the Haunted Cave.

"George died a couple of years ago. When they found him in the cave, he was smiling, looked like he had just gone to sleep. Everybody liked George, but they sure couldn't stand the tales he told about those dead people who visited him. I never saw Adele, but that day when I was with George and the kids, and he and the older boy saw her, and the boy tried to talk to her, it made a believer out of me. No, I've never seen a ghost."

I asked Earl if he had experienced any chills at the time Adele was said to be in the room?

"You bet, when they said Adele was in the room, then my hair stood up and I had chills, all up and down me."

It doesn't seem likely that any member of the family experienced the chills familiar with the manifestation of a "ghost." It would appear that a person newly dead still retains sufficient vital force to use for their own materialization. It is when they attempt later, perhaps months later, to materialize that it is necessary for them to draw on the energy from physically living beings.

Hey,
Look at Me

The old towns of Randsburg, Johannesburg, and Red Mountain, are well known in California, and in mining circles all over the country. Millions of dollars worth of gold and silver have been dug from their mines. The dumps containing the debris left after crushing the rock and extracting the ore are so huge as to look like mountains themselves. The old-timers still living there, and there aren't many of them, sit about the pot-bellied stoves and talk about the good old days, predicting they will return because the earth contains as much gold today as that which has been taken out. In fact, right now, a large American company has been conducting exploration, and word has it they will reopen one of the mines and work it.

In the days before the coming of the American miners, the Spanish had worked a mine called today "The Old Spanish Mine." It isn't known when it was abandoned, or given over to the Americans, but for many years it was worked by the gringos. One of those gringos was an artist and he drew a picture of the interior, or glory hole, of the mine. Glory hole is the name for a pocket of ore that is removed, leaving a large hole in the tunnel. The holes were so large that at times it was necessary to build scaffolding to support the top and sides lest they cave in. The miners usually spent their rest periods in the glory hole. The drawing was just that, miners sitting about in the glory hole. The family who owns the drawing now bought it about ten years ago to hang on the wall of their home.

It isn't known just when it first happened, but the family began to notice that the picture more often than not was cocked at an angle, or turned almost completely upside down. The wife was the first person to see what appeared to be the transparent shadow-picture of a Spanish miner superimposed on the face of the painting. When she had observed this phenomenon a couple of times, turning the picture many different ways to see what was causing it, she called it to the attention of the other members of the family, who also saw the old Spanish miner. The transparency was only seen when the picture had been cocked over, as though whoever was doing it was trying to draw attention by moving the picture so those present would notice it and then see him! When the picture was moved back to center the transparency disappeared.

Neighbors were called in from time to time to see for themselves. All of them saw it. The old Spaniard only appeared during the night hours. The family tried every way to prove that what they saw was a shadow, but despite their best efforts, the old boy kept appearing when he wanted to, not subject to their investigations.

Being such an historical area, many artists from around the country have stopped off in the three towns to paint scenes. The towns are separated by no more than a mile, so anything happening in one town is sure to be common knowledge in the other two. The word went out the family had a guest.

Expert artists studied the painting and made all kinds of tests on it to see what could possibly be causing the transparency of the Spaniard.

When the picture was upright he wasn't there. When the picture was tilted, and it was the proper time and condition, there he was!—but only after dark, or when the room was physically darkened. No other sign has been given the family they are host to a ghost, nothing but his likeness over the drawing of the glory hole. It seems that what he is trying to do is let them know he worked in that mine, that he is still around. He just wants to draw attention to himself.

If you should be in the vicinity of Randsburg, California, inquire about the portrait containing the old Spanish ghost.

A comedic side story concerns one of the better mines and how it was named. It seems the wife of the superintendent of a mine had taken a buggy trip to the town to the town of Mojave to do some shopping. On her way back, after wending up the road from the valley floor, she had a natural urge. There were no gas stations or comfort stations in those days, so she chose to disappear behind a large boulder.

During her concentration she noticed a rock that looked different than the others. Picking it up proved it of a great deal more weight than ordinary field stone. She completed her toilet, pocketed the rock, and drove on home. That evening when her husband got off work, she showed him the rock. He had it assayed and it was found to be high-grade, gold-silver ore. They returned to the spot where she'd found it, and staked a claim. The mine name they established for the site, laughingly, because of the manner in which it had been discovered, and because they didn't want to demean either the mine or the lady, was "The Yellow Aster!"

The Poor Farm
Ghost

This present-day phenomenon was encountered by Bill and Clair Brocket, Bridgeport, California, September 1968. Clair Brocket recorded it for me in their home, September 15, 1969, 10:40 A.M., in Bridgeport:

We live in Bridgeport, California, mostly in the summer time. Bill, my husband, and I, went for a ride out as far as Rasmussens, a trailer court along the highway on the way to the Bodie Road. It was around 9:30 at night, in September, last year, right about this time. On our way back, it was right near the Poor Farm; and we were driving along, there were no cars coming. It was a dark night, there was no moon. All of a sudden I saw something approaching the car, or, actually, the car was approaching it. It was on my side of the car, kinda off to one side, real close to the car. It was a flimsy bunch of white, and I got the definite impression of a face. I moved over to get away from it. I didn't say anything or make any outcry to Bill, because it happened so fast, and I felt kinda foolish to think I would see something.

Then Bill said, "What was that?"

I said, "Did you see it?"

"Yes. What did it look like to you?"

"It looked like something white, like white arms. It didn't have any hands but I think I saw a face. It was flimsy stuff."

"Did you feel the car hit anything?"

"No."

We had only been driving about thirty-five or forty miles an hour. Bill stopped the car, turned around and we went back to where we had seen this thing. We both got out of the car and began looking around with our flashlights. There was nothing there, anywhere around. There was no fog, no patches of ground haze or mist. The only way I can describe it is that you couldn't actually see a body. It was just flimsy stuff, but it had shape, it was transparent. It was white. It was large. It was three or four feet wide.

The only thing I can say was that it looked like what people always describe as a ghost. Now that sounds ridiculous, but it did have arms, it had a face, it had a shape, it was floating off the ground. It was about window high, about five feet off the ground.

We talked about it all the way back to the house, and even after we went to bed, we laid there and wondered what it could have been. The face kept haunting me. Bill hadn't seen the face. We wondered if we had come close enough to someone walking along to have knocked them further off the highway than we had looked. The next day we drove back out there and looked all over the place, in daylight. It was awful, it really scared both of us. I've never seen it again, and whenever I pass that spot, day or night, I always wait to see if we will see it again. It was right in front of the Poor Farm, and I said to Bill, "It must be a ghost from the Poor Farm, I wonder who it was?"

It wasn't imagination, because Bill saw it, too. It seemed like the stuff, whatever it was, came right up against the car. Bill said he saw it just off to the right of the car, in front of us. When I saw it, it was almost up against my window. The Poor Farm was where the poor people of the county lived when they get too old to work or take care of themselves. It was built about seventy years ago. Someone else owns it now; it's not being used as a poor farm, but they still call it that. I came here the first time in 1932, and have been coming back ever since. I've never seen anything like it before, we've never seen it since, and no one has told us they have seen anything like it. You hate to say anything to people because they either think you were drunk, or maybe you're a little nuts! Bill and I hadn't been drinking. It was there.

That is the end of the Brocket ghost story, but it brings up an interesting topic. The form of matter used in psychic communication such as we've just seen is called ectoplasm. It is matter, organized energy. It may assume a liquid, solid, or gaseous state; may appear as steam, ice, invisible vapor, or water. Ectoplasm has been observed, handled, and photographed; it has been weighed. The substance has been drawn into rods, levers, and other objects. It has been observed and photographed exuding from the body of those sleeping or entranced mediums capable of emitting ectoplasm. Where ectoplasmic exudations have been observed, particularly in a closed room, there has been a noticeable drop in the room temperature.

Ectoplasm is known to be a substance from which materializations are possible by excarnate spirits. Remember the chills reported by Florence ("I'm Still with You"), and by many of those who've experienced materializations? The drop in temperature has been attributed to the exudation, however manufactured, as using the vital force of incarnate persons. There is as much experimenting on the other side by the excarnates as there is on this side by us! Perhaps more.

Knitting
in the Graveyard

Graveyard stories keep popping up. Those two fine people, Grace Brandon and her brother, John Sturgeon, of Bridgeport, California, contributed this one.

When they were children they lived in the then booming town of Bodie. Their mother had a woman friend, Margaret, who lived in Hawthorne, Nevada, about thirty miles away. Margaret had a flock of kids, and frequently she would pile them into a spring wagon and take them along when she went to Bodie to visit the Sturgeons. People in those areas thought no more of making a sixty-mile trip in a wagon than we do of a 150-mile trip in a car today. Even today's residents of the Sierras don't judge distance by the mile, but rather, they say it will take so much time to reach their destination.

Margaret agitatedly reported to Mrs. Sturgeon that on many occasions when she passed the graveyard in the late afternoon, like around 4 o'clock, as she and the kids were heading back down to Hawthorne, she saw the distinct but transparent figure of a woman near one particular gravestone; the figure was suspended in midair. The woman was always knitting. She was dressed in white, her head bent, watching what she was doing.

If this phenomenon had happened only once it could have

been chalked up to imagination, mist, reflection, or whatever, but it happened a number of times when Margaret passed by. It got to the point where Margaret and her brood would leave Bodie very early in the afternoon, so she wouldn't see the "ghost." If she did overstay, she remained overnight with her family, then returned to Hawthorne the following day. This didn't set well with her husband because lacking a telephone or other instant communication he would ride out to see if she and the kids were alright.

Margaret finally became so disturbed at the apparition that she stopped going to Bodie at all. Two other Bodieites reported without prompting that they also saw the apparition, and upon comparing notes with Margaret, they found their observations checked in every detail. I asked Vicky Cain, that former resident of Bodie, if he'd ever heard of the knitting woman? Yes, he had heard of her but had not seen her.

Grace reports that records show the person buried under that gravestone was a man who'd died of natural causes quite a few years before Margaret ever saw the ghostly woman visitor. The only conclusion any of them could come to was that for some reason the apparition seemed to want to be close to the man whom she had perhaps either been married to or in love with; or could it have been his sister or mother? If it was a sweetheart who was maintaining vigil, was she hoping one day he would return, in spirit also, to find her waiting for him?

Or, who knows? Is it the memory tape of time replaying? Or the memory tape of the knitting woman herself?

The question has been asked many times about how widespread the belief in ghosts is? From my own investigations and a check of the percentages, indications are that eight out of ten people believe there is something to ghosts and psychic phenomena; half the people approached in my travels about the country knew of "things" which have happened to others, and half that number report personal experiences.

On January 15, 1970, I was asked to appear on a popular, local, daytime, home-audience-participation TV show. During my chats with the show's host I made mention of this book. We had a lively discussion of ghosts, and with the host's permission I asked the home audience to send me stories or anecdotes about ghostly phenomena they'd heard about or which had occurred to them. Before the show was over the secretaries and switchboard operator came into the studio to report a total of eight people calling in, they didn't want to wait to write a letter!

I called them back later that day, and after listening to their tales, obtained permission to relate their phenomenon if I wanted to. I'd also asked the home audience to include written permission for me to possibly use their stories if they lent themselves to my format, which they all did, with the exception of one woman who wrote that my pursuance and belief in ghosts was the practice and belief in demonology; I would be hounded to the grave; the Bible forbids anyone messing around with psychic phenomena or ghosts of departed souls! The show was on a Thursday, and two days later, Saturday, the studio called asking me when I wanted to pick up the mail I had waiting for me—a total of twenty-six letters.

Most of the people gave me permission to include their stories, a couple did not. Here is a story I particularly liked.

"They're Around Your Shoulders"

Mrs. Kay, of Sepulveda, California, was having her troubles. Her thirty-seven-year-old husband was a very sick man and the doctor had told them both he would have to be moved to a hospital, perhaps for a long time. Mrs. Kay's plight was all the worse because the couple had four children, ranging from one year to fourteen years, and Mr. Kay was the only means of support. A friend of hers knew of a woman reputed to be a psychic, and persuaded Mrs. Kay to visit her. They called and made an appointment. The moment they walked into the psychic's living room, the woman came to Mrs. Kay with out-stretched hands saying, "Oh, my dear, you have great trouble." They seated themselves around the coffee table in the living room, and the woman continued to talk to Mrs. Kay.

"Your husband is very ill. I see him being moved to a room with a very low bed. I wonder why the bed is so low?"

The psychic never looked directly at Mrs. Kay, which was disconcerting, and Mrs. Kay finally asked her what she was looking at over her shoulders?

"You have the spirits of two people close to you, who are with you now. They are speaking to me with their thoughts, and I am telling you what I receive. From his smile and his closeness to you I believe one of the spirits was your father. The other one you knew when they were in life, I do not know who they are. It is a woman."

"Where are those spirits?"

"They are around your shoulders, they do not touch you. Your father will speak to you, soon. He is trying to talk to you."

That sitting was on a Saturday. The following Wednesday Mr. Kay was moved to the hospital by ambulance. When Mrs. Kay walked into his hospital room that afternoon, the first thing she noted was that he was in a bed "lower than any I'd ever seen in a hospital. It was like they had cut off the legs of the bed to lower it."

Mr. Kay was quite pitiable with his pleas that he not be left in the hospital. He kept repeating that if she left him there he knew he would never walk out; he couldn't stand it.

That night when Mrs. Kay went to bed, about 11:30, she lay there asking for direction and help. Suddenly it seemed to her she heard a familiar voice telling her to get out of bed and get on her knees. She distinctly heard the voice tell her three times to get out of bed, get on her knees and pray. After the third time she did get on her knees at bedside and pray. There was no further audible voice, but she felt she was not alone in the room.

An hour later she was awakened by a call from the hospital telling her that her husband had suddenly relapsed, that he had died at 11:30 P.M. When she hung up the phone she just sat there, numb, unthinking. Then she heard the voice again and she knew this time it was the voice of her father who had passed on many years ago. He was telling her that Mr. Kay was now with them, that he was out of pain, he would have passed on no matter what they had done for him at the hospital, it was his time to go. Her father also told her that Mr. Kay would communicate with her directly when he had recovered from the experience of going to the other side, when he had fully awakened.

Ten days after the funeral, Mrs. Kay's fourteen-year-old daughter came to her mother and told her that for two days now she had thought she saw her father in the room, near the closet, that he was there now. They both started for the girl's room, and were joined by the eight-year-old brother. When the three entered the room, the boy pointed to the closet and said, "Look, there's dad."

Sure enough, dad was there. It was as though a transparent portrait had been printed on the door of the closet. It was a half figure, from the waist up, and he was smiling. The boy ran over to the closet and put out his hand to touch the portrait, and it disappeared. A week later the transparency returned to the closet door to be seen by the girl and Mrs. Kay and then disappeared. The figure of Mr. Kay has not returned since then.

About a month after the husband's death, Mrs. Kay returned for a sitting with the psychic, who upon hearing of Mr. Kay's death, showed Mrs. Kay her diary, with a note on the day of the first visit, a note she'd made at the time saying, "Mr. Kay will die, shortly." She told Mrs. Kay she was not permitted to tell her at the time of the impending death, but she had known of it.

"She Likes
Our Daughter, Tina"

It is most refreshing to meet people who live day in and day out with a ghost, and it doesn't seem to bother them, most of them. In fact, they get a kick out of it. I might add, they feel sorry for the ghost, because one member of the family used to know her. The ghost is a little girl, about ten or eleven.

Jack and Barbara Meyers, their nineteen-year-old daughter, Tina, eight-year-old Kelly, and seventeen-year-old Kevin live in Northridge, California, and although they weren't a bit hesitant about letting me use their real names, they did ask that I not reveal the house number or the street. They've taken their phone number out of the book because of so many calls once the phenomena came to light. The house is a hangout for both teenagers and adults, and word travels fast when a haunting is occurring.

In 1942 Jack was living with his grandmother in Burbank. It was just prior to World War II. The grandmother was taking care of a mentally retarded child. The girl, Carmen, had been the daughter of a close friend of the grandmother, and when the woman's husband was killed in an automobile accident, Carmen, as they say, "flipped out," and the grandmother was taking care of her while the mother worked in another part of the state. No doubt, prior to the emotional trauma of losing her father, Carmen had been emotionally ill, and the death of the father slid her over the line, but it hadn't been evident until the death.

Jack says she was described by the doctors as a psychomotor epileptic, which they know more about today than they did then. To put it bluntly, people said the child had fits, which to all outward appearances she did. Carmen took quite a fancy to Jack during his stay at his grandmother's. For the four months before Jack entered the Army, he and Carmen were together a great deal; she'd substituted Jack for the dead father; they became very close. Jack was in the service for a considerable period of time, as most of us were, and he heard from the grandmother that Carmen had been placed in the state hospital at Camarillo, California, for the mentally and emotionally disturbed.

When Jack returned to civilian life, he visited his grandmother and inquired about Carmen, learning that she had died during one of her seizures, in the hospital, when she was about eleven years old.

A few years later Jack's grandfather passed on; Jack got married and bought the house in which he, Barbara, and the family now live. The grandmother, now reaching an advanced age, has sold her house and moved in with Jack's mother. Jack and Barbara received a large portion of the furnishings and the furniture the grandmother had. Two of those pieces of furniture were rocking chairs: one upholstered, with an ottoman, the other a black-stained, walnut rocker, about one hundred years old; and we will hear more about them as the story progresses. The upholstered rocker was placed in the living room, the other in their daughter Tina's room.

Almost at once, after receiving the articles, things started happening. Neither Jack nor Barbara had ever had any contact with a ghost, had merely heard stories like the rest of us. Let Barbara tell of her first encounter.

"One night I had gone to bed, and I was just sitting there in the dark, and suddenly I just knew there was someone in the room with me. The first thing I thought of was, prowler." She turned on the light and looked around.

"There, by the bookcase, in front of it, stood this condensed fog. I say stood, but that's what it was doing, just standing there. Jack, who'd been asleep, woke up and right away he said, "There's something in this room, I feel it, I can see it.' I said, 'I can see it. Where do you *think* it is?' Jack said, 'It's right in front of the bookcase,' and I said, 'That's right. What does it look like?' and he said, 'Fog, or mist,' and with that it disappeared."

Neither one of them mentioned anything to the kids about having a visitation by a patch of fog; they didn't want to upset them. Shortly thereafter, when Barbara was again lying in bed, she felt "someone" or "something" press on her hand, like another hand. She opened her eyes, and just knowing there was someone in there, said, "All right. I'll admit you're here." With that she turned on the light and looked around. The ball or patch of fog was in front of the bookcase again, but this time it was twirling, revolving fast. She said, "All right, who are you?" She says she then received the mental impression of a young girl named Carmen, a girl with long, dark, curly hair. She said to the fog, "Are you trying to communicate with me?" and it disappeared.

Not long after that, Tina, then about fifteen, told her mother she didn't like to go into her room, because one day when she was in there brushing her hair, she thought Kevin, then about thirteen, was hiding in the closet, watching her.

She went to the closet and opened it and called for him to come out. She moved the clothes back and could find nothing. Tina knew there was nothing in there, but she also knew "something" was.

About three weeks later, Barbara had taken a shower, put on her robe, and was walking back down the hall to the master bedroom, when she distinctly felt a tap on her shoulder. She turned around, thinking one of the kids had sneaked up on her, but nobody was in the hall with her. Barbara thought it was her imagination, and continued on down the hall, almost immediately there were now two taps on her shoulder. She didn't know what to do about it, so she just walked into the bedroom, and it didn't happen again.

A few days after that, Barbara walked into the front room and there was their Laborador retriever, Baby, standing in the middle of the floor, her hackles up, growling ominously, looking at the overstuffed rocking chair. She isn't known to growl at adults but she definitely doesn't like kids, and growls when they are near her, warns them off. The rocker wasn't moving, no.

One night Jack was awakened by what he thought was one of the kids falling out of bed. He got up and went up the hall to see which one it was. As he walked down the hall, footsteps walked right by him! As Jack says, "That shook me." No one touched him, just walked right by. That was about three years ago.

The manifestations, or visitations, seem to take place in cycles. They occur frequently for a period of time, then stop for awhile. To borrow from the Atwood story, perhaps the Meyer's ghost has to take a vacation, get recharged, rejuvenated. It could be very tiring for them, trying to make contact with these dense physical entities here on the earth plane, as difficult for the spirits to make contact with us as vice versa. The Meyers have never charted or kept notes on the periods of occurrence of the phenomena. At the time, as they say, those things which happen seem so normal, just seem to happen. Anyhow, they were getting quite a reputation as those "Nutty Meyers!" A very discerning girl at the office where Barbara works, after hearing tales of the goings-on in their house, said she received the impression it all had something to do with Jack's side of the family. (Every woman likes to hear that!) It was then Barbara asked Jack if he'd ever known a little girl named Carmen.

"My word, I haven't thought of that child in years. Why?"

"Did she have long, dark hair, kinda natural curly? Was she around eleven or twelve?"

"Yes."

"Well, that's who it is then."

And there it seems we have possibly the name and the background of our ghost.

Another night Barbara, Tina, Kevin, and Kelly were sitting in the front room on the davenport; Barbara was seated on the ottoman in front of the overstuffed rocker. Barbara can pick up the incident from here.

"Well, I heard who I thought was Jack come walking down the hall behind me and sit down in the rocker. I turned to say something to him, and that rocker was rocking, and there wasn't anyone in it or even near it. It was rocking violently, not just a little bit. It has a definite creak we all know, and it was creaking up a storm. That kind of startled me, and I took off that ottoman right now, like I'd been shot. The kids all saw it and they had their eyes bugged out."

It is much more evidential when a manifestation is observed collectively, others are in on it. None of the four in the room had been talking about any of the ghostly happenings, they were discussing daily affairs. Ghosts were the furthest things from their minds, so they couldn't have been collectively influencing a mass manifestation.

The rocker in daughter Tina's room goes a-rocking quite frequently. Jack says he has always been a "skeptical believer." He has checked the floor in Tina's bedroom, gone into the attic for three days, with a builder along with him, to try and find anything which might possibly cause any of the strange happenings.

The ghost, Carmen, if you will, does frequent the attic at times, and she knocks and bangs all around; so Jack wanted the attic professionally gone over for any loose fittings, connections, pipes, etc., but found everything tight and ship-shape. All of the attic noises seem to occur over the hall or the bathroom, and especially over Tina's room. The whole family has heard the noises from the attic; they can be heard all over the house. When Kelly hears it he hollers, "There she goes again!" The noises in the attic come and go as do the other manifestations by Carmen.

The kids and Barbara brought Tina's rocker out into the front room one night for a seance. After the seance got under way, the rocker began going, with Tina in it, then a light appeared under it, getting larger and larger. Tina came forward in the chair, sitting on the edge of it. The rocking finally became so violent the chair went over backwards with a crash, Tina exiting just in time. One of the legs was broken when it went over. Everyone split; the seance was over!

Carmen also hums and sings, very low, just a few bars or lines of a song. Around 1940, when Carmen was staying with Jack's grandmother, Ella Fitzgerald made a hit record called "A Tisket, A Tasket," and it was on radio constantly. Carmen, of course, picked it up and hummed or sang parts of it, particularly "a tisket, a tasket, a green and yellow basket." Those are the words the Meyers hear; all of them have heard it when Carmen is in her singing mood. That singing also helped nail down that it was Carmen who was living under the same roof with them.

Just two nights before I talked with the Meyers, Tina had awakened in the middle of the night and heard the singing. She thought at first she might have been singing in her sleep, but the tuneless tune continued, nothing identifiable, just aimless humming, loud, *da-da, da, da-da-da.* Tina said it was the loudest she'd ever heard it.

At another time, one evening, Barbara and Tina were sitting at a table they have in the nook adjoining the kitchen; Kevin was standing by it. Suddenly they heard a noise and looked into the kitchen. The cupboard door, up high over the main section of the cupboard, flew open and a large glass bowl came sailing out into the air, bounced down on the sink top, bounded into the air, and fell to the floor. Except when it hit there wasn't the expected crash; it was more gently accomplished, as though someone had dropped the bowl and had caught it before it hit the floor and broke. There wasn't a scratch on it, not a nick. I saw the bowl, looked it over carefully.

Kevin, the seventeen-year-old is the only one in the family who gets "spooky" about the manifestations—about the whole thing, actually. Kelly, the eight-year-old, rather takes it all in stride. He sat during the entire interview, his big blue eyes wide open, shining, eager, knowing.

Once, when Kelly was about four, he had come running into the kitchen and told his mother that "twirly" was in the living room. He'd not heard the conversations about Carmen during her seizures, when, just prior to one of them, she would begin going around in a circle, faster and faster, until she was literally *twirling;* then she would drop to the floor in a catatonic state for some minutes. As has been mentioned before, the kids are closer to the other side than we adults. They accept more without question that which scares us, makes us doubt our sanity, or our eyes, or ears when an entity from the other side tries to manifest. I asked Kelly what he thought about all this, and he said, "It's O.K." And I knew he meant it. It doesn't bother him at all. He laughed delightedly when I asked him if it scared him. "Naww."

I keep saying, "Another time...." But that's exactly how it was related to me. All the Meyers would interject with "Another time...." What's an author to do?

Anyhow, "another time," Tina was in her bedroom, sitting in front of the dresser fixing her hair. Barbara was seated on the bed; Kevin was standing near the hall door, with his back to the clothes closet. The closet door was open, and one of Tina's dresses was hanging in there on a hanger. Barbara got the impression out of the corner of her eye that the dress was moving, and she looked over at it. It *were!* Barbara said, "Kevin, look behind you." Kevin took one look, jumped clear out the door of the bedroom, and split for the front. Kevin doesn't dig Carmen, or any other ghost.

Sometime back Carmen decided to inhabit Tina's room. She has an affinity for Tina. We were in luck. Tina, who'd been visiting a friend in the hospital, popped in the front door. She is about the prettiest, bursting nineteen-year-old it's been my extreme pleasure to see since the blonde bombshell Veronica Lake hit the silver screen with such dramatic impact back in the 1940s. Clean, fresh, vigorous, balanced, knowledgeable, well-mannered, provocative. I like her! She got right into the middle of the conversation, like an old pro, and took over, and this is how it went. Me first.

"Tina, what do you think about all this ghost bit?"

"Cool. Carmen's a nice little girl. I wish I could see her, talk to her. You know, I feel sorry for her. I know about her past life, when she was alive, and she's very sad, I think. She seems just to want to be with someone she likes. I wonder if people have much to do with each other on the other side? Are they friendly?"

That was for openers. Then we went into the details of what's happened or what's happening to Tina now.

"Oh, I was fixing my hair last week, and I'd just put my hands down from my head, and whuupp, up went some strands of it, in back, here—about a half a handful just stood straight up, then slowly fell back down in place."

"Did that scare you, Tina?"

"Nope. I talk to her when I know she's in the room with me. Like you would talk to a friend. That reminds me. One day I came home and walked in the front room, and I thought I saw a friend of mine, Diane, walking in the hallway, pass the front room hall door, and go into my bedroom. She's over here a lot, so I just went on into the kitchen. I didn't hear anything from her, so I called to her, 'Diane, what are you doing?' and there was no answer so I went in the bedroom, and she wasn't there. I thought maybe she was playing tricks so I looked under the bed, in the closet, in the bathroom, all over. Then I remembered she didn't have on the right clothes. The girl I saw was wearing oxfords, a longer skirt than we wear today, with a jacket. So then I knew it must be Carmen, and I hoped I would see her again, but I didn't."

"Another time," Tina was sitting at the nook table just off

the kitchen, with curlers and bobby pins in her hair. Barbara was present, as was Kelly. Without touching her head, a curler from each side unrolled itself, and was gently deposited on the table in front of Tina, along with a number of bobby pins. The pins seemed to present some difficulty, and you could "see" invisible fingers fumbling, loosening them, to place them in a small pile on the table by the curlers.

Many of Kevin's friends have been watching TV in the middle of the afternoon, when the big, overstuffed rocker in the living room will begin to rock. Jack, being a skeptical believer, has recently moved the rocker back against the wall, wedged it up against the couch, where it would have a difficult time rocking. I personally would go ahead and let Carmen rock, poor kid, but to each his own. I don't live with the phenomenon. Maybe I'd get tired hearing a squeaky rocker, hour after hour, even with someone in it, let alone "empty!"

At night, many times, everyone has heard the footsteps in the hall. I asked if the footsteps had shoes on, and they said no; but then the hall is carpeted. It's just footsteps.

Jack was awakened out of a sound sleep one night and got up to wander around and see if the kids were all right. He was walking down the hall, again, and he saw "this girl." She was dressed the way they dressed in the 1940s. She didn't say anything, but turned and went into the wall, *poof.* He wasn't scared, but rather, disturbed! The bathroom light was on because Tina at that time insisted they keep it so. I wonder if it was for Carmen, or because even Tina, Carmen's friend, was a bit queazy about walking down dark halls, never knowing if she would "walk through her?" The apparition was very definitely a "person." Carmen was, that time, wearing a dark dress, dark blue, or dark red, Jack couldn't really tell, but it had white trim, and was quite lengthy, as they wore dresses then, big girls as well as little girls. Jack said that although he professes to being skeptical, as long as I was levelling about getting the story for publication, he would level: "I did see it. It was a girl. It could have been Carmen. I don't know. It walked into the wall, so I knew it wasn't any living person I knew, and it was dressed the way I said." Jack admitted before I left that only recently has he become thoroughly convinced that someone, Carmen perhaps, is there, definitely.

"Another time," Tina was standing at the kitchen sink doing some of her laundry. She glanced down and saw a pair of men's shoes and a portion of trouser legs (like the Atwoods). She thought it was her dad, and she shook her hands off, turned around. No one was there, in fact, no one else was in the house. A man's shoes, and trousers? Tina has received the definite impression that there is a man present as she's seen the same thing two other times. She thinks it is a man who has had some connection with the family, like her grandfather. He died when Tina was six months old. She's never seen the face belonging to the shoes and trousers, but she feels she might one day.

The last time Tina saw Carmen, the apparition had dark hair, wore a jumper-type dress with puffy sleeves, and oxfords. As Tina said, "I just sorta freaked when I saw her, but she was there for about thirty seconds."

If it is Carmen, she does talk, and has been heard by any number of people, guests included. Usually the talk consists of "Mommy, Mommy," loud; and sometimes, clearly, "Tina." This happens frequently, in every quarter of the house. And of course, her "a tisket, a tasket." Tina has sung along with her, in hopes of establishing more contact with her. It hasn't worked so far, but who knows?

There has been a "cold spot" in Tina's room for a long time. It's just an area, invisibly outlined, which is degrees colder than any other portion of the room. One night Tina, in her nightgown, went over and stood in the cold spot. I'll let her tell it.

"My whole nightgown went *wooomm*, billowed up and out all around me. My girl friend, who was staying with me, blew her mind, and went screaming out of the room. She freaked out."

"She looks about ten, but she's big for her age, Carmen. She hasn't been smiling when I've seen her, but she wasn't sad looking. I guess she just looked curious, and then she does giggle. She giggled when I saw her the last time, and put her hand up to her mouth. She peeks out from behind stuff, like a kid that age, playing games. I guess she knows where she is."

So you won't become bored(!) with any more tales of Carmen, let me get this one down because of its rarity, even amongst ghost hunters.

Tina was awakened one night by something fussing around her feet. She was sleeping on her stomach, and before she became fully awake, she was bodily flipped over on her back. That brought her bolt upright, and there, floating before her, about a foot out in front of her face, was a pink rose, stem, thorns, and all. Let her finish it.

"Yeah, well it's wild. I felt something flip me over. I didn't do it myself. Then I sat up, wondering what in the world happened. Right there in front of me was a beautiful rose, and the stem, and I could see the thorns, it was that close. I didn't smell it, but it was pink. It floated around for a little bit then just disappeared. It was really weird. Then she pulled the covers off me. She's done that a lot of times."

Actually, I could go on, page after page, but I'd rather hoard the rest of the material on the Meyers/Carmen ghost for another time, as the evidence mounts. And perhaps Carmen will materialize long enough to be able to converse, tell her story about what it is like "over there." It's possible, and the longer I pursue the concept of continuing life, the more possible and plausible I find it becoming. We'll get to the place, one day, where verbal communication with our discarnates could be as common as leaning over the back fence and talking to a neighbor. When that happens I want to be present, taking it all down on my tape recorder!

For the astrology fans, here are the birth dates for the Meyers.

Jack Meyers, born February 28, 1923, Glendale, California, at 11:55 P.M.

Barbara Meyers, born November 15, 1923, Alhambra, California, no time given.

Tina Meyers, born June 26, 1951, 11:55 A.M., Glendale, California.

Kevin Meyers is a Pisces.

Kelly Meyers is a Libran.

I have taken the liberty of using the name and title of Freda Morris, Ph.D., assistant professor of medical psychology at the UCLA Neuropsychiatric Institute, in reference to some of the various people she has directed me to for their stories, including the Meyers family, and now I would like to put down her answer to my question about the veracity, stability, and/or pathology she found when the individuals were tested by her.

"I have given psychological tests to some of the people mentioned in this book. I have found that the tests showed essentially normal personalities. There is not sufficient pathology in any of these cases to suggest hallucination as an explanation for the phenomena. There must be an energy form yet to be discovered, which, when found, will make these psychic phenomena tenable and will fit them into the framework of our scientific world view."

Thank you, Laurie
Richard Webb